Second Century Believers

Second Century Believers

by
Deborah Clark Vance

George Ronald
Oxford

George Ronald, *Publisher*
Oxford
www.grbooks.com

© Deborah Clark Vance 2024
All Rights Reserved

*A catalogue record for this book is available
from the British Library*

ISBN 978–0–85398–670–6

I dedicate this book to the
steadfast second century believers

Contents

Acknowledgments	ix
Introduction	1
1 Early Christians	4
2 First Century American Bahá'ís	17
Election of the Universal House of Justice	29
The Nine Year Plan	34
3 The Sixties	35
Living in the USA	41
Society	43
Race	53
Religion	57
Culture	64
Search for Truth	74
Reason	77
Feelings	88
Inspiration	94
Intuition	99
Awakening/Conversion	108
Discovery	115
Fulfillment	116
4 Second Century Believers	120
Relationships with First Century Bahá'ís	127
Persian Bahá'í Refugees	143
Engagement	153
Remaining Active	168
5 Truth, Community, Service, Spirit	176
Truth	177

Community	179
Service	182
Spirit	182
Spiritual Forces	185
Afterword	189
Glossary	192
Bibliography	213
References	221

Acknowledgments

I could not have written this book without those individuals who generously shared their personal thoughts and feelings about entering the Bahá'í community and remaining actively engaged for the past five decades. I also wish to thank my husband Steve for coming up with a more perfect phrasing here and there. Finally, in 1970 when we both worked at the US Bahá'í National Center, I never would have dreamed that 54 years later I'd be working with my talented and insightful editor, Wendi Momen.

Introduction

A great many youth who did not grow up in Bahá'í families entered the Bahá'í Faith between 1964 and 1973. Although there were those who withdrew from membership or stayed out of touch, a strong cohort of others are still actively engaged in Bahá'í communities; I count myself among them. This book presents voices of US Americans who were in their teens or early twenties when they became Bahá'ís and have been active believers for the past half century or so. I wanted to explore how the social environment during that eventful decade had influenced this generation's thought processes while seeking and accepting the Bahá'í Faith, and what has enabled them to remain actively engaged in it even a half century later, at the time of writing.

Expectations were high for this generation from both their elders and the Faith. The first plan of the first Universal House of Justice was progress. Many of the youth who responded as international pioneers have spent their lives serving in distant lands, away from their families of origin and their native language and culture. The book that looks back on the 20th century, *Century of Light*, notes, 'No segment of the community made a more energetic or significant contribution to this dramatic process of growth than did Bahá'í youth.'[1]

I have frequently studied groups of people throughout my professional career, using qualitative research procedures. I've used some of its tools for gathering and organizing personal information because such procedures offer a systematic way to examine people's feelings and experiences to find common themes which provide a snapshot of group members.

First, however, I explore the state of Christianity in its second century so as later to compare and contrast its early development with that of the Bahá'í Faith. I selected Christianity for comparison because we know little about the lives of second-century believers back then. Then I look at the Bahá'í Faith in the United States during its first century. Many Bahá'í histories and biographies are written about these earliest American believers who were groundbreaking in the development of the Faith. I follow with a look at the reality of the 1964–1973 period and weave the accounts of Bahá'ís who during that time were reacting to their social and political environment, questioning their churches and looking for spiritual answers. Although the term 'culture of learning' didn't become widespread until the end of the 20th century, it has always been true of members of the Bahá'í Faith which has no clergy and expects its members to read and study its scripture.

While much of the history of the Bahá'í Faith in the United States and its adherents has focused on first-century developments in the religion and on significant individuals who were instrumental in its growth, I wanted to focus instead on those who helped carry forward the work in the next century, the Formative Age, when the 'firsts' had been accomplished. I therefore interviewed a specific cohort who became Bahá'ís in a specific time period. I used a systematic approach to gather and digest first-person accounts of their feelings and experiences, starting with the time they were seeking, and then accepting, Bahá'u'lláh's station as true. I look at how such internal experience may have been influenced by current events in the 1960s. As a Bahá'í who shares the same demographics and experienced the same time period as my respondents, I'm a participant-observer. My interview questions are drawn from my experiences and observations during this time period. I also look at studies about conversions into Christianity during the same decade.

Working on this project, new – perhaps unanswerable – questions came to mind, having to do with the workings of spirit. What are spiritual forces? Were they released when the

INTRODUCTION

House of Justice was elected? Were they released by the Ten Year Crusade and the first Nine Year Plan? What spiritual influence on the young did the older believers effect – people who had met 'Abdu'l-Bahá and Shoghi Effendi, those who served as Hands of the Cause, or even those whose parents had lived during the days of Bahá'u'lláh and the Báb? I suspect that spiritual powers *were* released at that time that churned things up. I present writings on the subject and examine how they might apply to the way events unfolded. In its Foreword to *Century of Light*, the Universal House of Justice writes,

> The conclusion of the twentieth century provides Bahá'ís with a unique vantage point. During the past hundred years our world underwent changes far more profound than any in its preceding history, changes that are, for the most part, little understood by the present generation. These same hundred years saw the Bahá'í Cause emerge from obscurity, demonstrating on a global scale the unifying power with which its Divine origin has endowed it. As the century drew to its close, the convergence of these two historical developments became increasingly apparent.[2]

I
Early Christians

What if we could read accounts from second-century Christians about how they lived and worshipped? Would they reveal teachings of Jesus that weren't included in the Gospel? Even as church dogma and organization were still being formulated, certain early Christian authors were branded heretical and others deemed orthodox. Scrutiny of the writings from that period began in greater earnest with the discovery of ancient scrolls – 13 Gnostic books – in Nag Hammadi, Egypt, in 1945.[1] It is thought that some of the forbidden writings had been buried to save them from destruction. Interestingly, some present-day Christians have been influenced by the content of these scrolls, such as the American Franciscan priest Richard Rohr who sends subscribers a popular daily newsletter about the spiritual practices of early Christians, whom he calls the desert fathers and mothers.[2]

Of course, the Bahá'í writings have been well preserved. We know their authenticity, so that won't become a concern unless and until any lost, stolen or forged Tablets were to emerge. The Faith's organization, under the guidance and direction of Shoghi Effendi and the Universal House of Justice, has been highly systematic and deliberate, so the chance is slim for counterfeit writings to break through.

The Bahá'í Faith has an Administrative Order whose grassroots character allows every member, at least each month at the Nineteen Day Feast, to consult and voice an opinion about how their community operates and to suggest plans, and generally share ideas. The local spiritual assemblies are elected yearly to oversee local business and the well-being of the wider community and are described by Shoghi Effendi as 'the chief sinews of Bahá'í society, as well as the ultimate foundation of its administrative structure'.[3] Indeed, the Feast is designed so that every community member has the opportunity to speak up, contribute ideas and consult about projects they and others are engaging in. Such a system relies on each and every individual to steep themselves in the teachings by reading, praying and meditating on guidance from the Central Figures and Shoghi Effendi as well as the Universal House of Justice.

Further, Shoghi Effendi has said,

> Let us also bear in mind that the keynote of the Cause of God is not dictatorial authority but humble fellowship, not arbitrary power, but the spirit of frank and loving consultation. Nothing short of the spirit of a true Bahá'í can hope to reconcile the principles of mercy and justice, of freedom and submission, of the sanctity of the right of the individual and of self-surrender, of vigilance, discretion and prudence on the one hand, and fellowship, candor and courage on the other.[4]

The practice of consultation is elucidated in the writings. Individuals at Feast meetings are enjoined to present ideas which are aligned with the teachings of the Faith. In short, there are numerous safeguards against power-seeking individuals taking over any aspect of Bahá'í administration.

Bahá'ís sometimes refer to themselves as the 'generation of the half-light',[5] conscious that the Faith is still in its infancy and that in the future our institutions as well as spiritual understanding will have evolved into something much different than they are today. But the religion is also emerging from obscurity and can celebrate the tremendous strides made during the past 178 years. Bahá'ís reside in all corners of the world, have established 179 National Spiritual Assemblies and translated the writings into more than 800 languages and counting. Over 500 primary texts have been translated from Persian and Arabic into English and many into other major languages as well. The

Bahá'í International Community has consultative status at the United Nations. Bahá'ís have built Houses of Worship on every continent except Antarctica and an array of buildings and gardens in Haifa and its environs. The Universal House of Justice has devised plans for the past 60 years. In the United States, the National Assembly issues monthly 'feast letters' in English, Spanish and Persian.

I thought it would be beneficial to record the thoughts of second-century Bahá'ís as a way of expressing some of the early boots-on-the-ground progress of the Bahá'í Faith. Because I am a second-century Bahá'í who grew up Christian, I've often wondered what second-century Christians might have felt and how their experiences compare to the way Bahá'ís feel today. One of the few things we know about actual life during early Christianity is that the people were mostly illiterate.

Whereas second-century Christians had lacked a coherent structure and official scripture, Bahá'u'lláh has provided inspired guidance for the formation of Bahá'í institutions. Nonetheless, as human beings, we are less spiritually evolved than our descendants will be in the future and we may be following our guidance in a less than perfect way. Surely, they will view us as primitive. And those future Bahá'ís may want to know some of the thought processes of us early Bahá'ís and be able to mark progress as they compare their thinking to ours today. By comparison, Christians know little about what their religion was like during its second century.

To establish an equivalent timeline between Christianity and the Bahá'í Faith, it's necessary to consider the beginning of Christianity as the time Jesus received His Revelation.

> The circumstances in which the Vehicle of this newborn Revelation, following with such swiftness that of the Báb, received the first intimations of His sublime mission recall, and indeed surpass in poignancy the soul-shaking experience of Moses when confronted by the Burning Bush in the wilderness of Sinai; of Zoroaster when awakened to His mission by a succession of seven visions; of Jesus when

coming out of the waters of the Jordan He saw the heavens opened and the Holy Ghost descend like a dove and light upon Him; of Muḥammad when in the Cave of Hira, outside of the holy city of Mecca, the voice of Gabriel bade Him 'cry in the name of Thy Lord'; and of the Báb when in a dream He approached the bleeding head of the Imám Ḥusayn, and, quaffing the blood that dripped from his lacerated throat, awoke to find Himself the chosen recipient of the outpouring grace of the Almighty.[6]

Estimates are that Jesus began His ministry sometime between 26 and 28 CE – with His crucifixion estimated to have been 36 CE – preaching to a Jewish population that expected the appearance of their Messiah. They had long been brutally oppressed by a barbaric, pagan Roman Empire that had kept them too illiterate and poor to have any more than a crude, literal understanding about Him even a hundred years after He had been cruelly executed. Because the Jews had expected their Messiah to free them from Roman oppression by force, Jesus was not considered to be the Messiah. The one notable exception was Gamaliel, a principal Jewish spiritual leader who, though largely ignored, had been the mentor of the apostle Paul.[7] He seemed to have sensed something about Jesus and perceived something special about Jesus' cause, cautioning his supporters not to persecute His followers.[8] 'Abdu'l-Bahá says Judas Iscariot 'became a cause of the crucifixion of that glorious Lord',[9] remarking in a talk in New York in 1912, 'Judas Iscariot had become a traitor and hypocrite'.[10] Of Caiaphas, Bahá'u'lláh wrote: 'Both Annas, the most learned among the divines of His day, and Caiaphas, the high priest, denounced Him and pronounced the sentence of His death.'[11]

Imagine what happens when a Manifestation of God appears amid a population which is not only without means, but illiterate. Think about the challenges of record-keeping. Surely Jesus shared concepts that were difficult to understand with people who couldn't read or write but tried their best to remember the phrases. Many things He proclaimed may never have been recorded and bits were remembered or misremembered. William V. Harris asserts a ten per cent literacy rate for the ancient world generally that has been qualified but overwhelmingly affirmed. The words of Jesus weren't recorded and were often taken literally rather than symbolically, however many of His teachings were shared orally and eventually written down. Because the Jews had expected a deliverer who would free them from Roman oppression by force, Jesus was not considered to be their Messiah.

Why would anyone want to follow a poor, homeless man who had been deemed by most religious and social leaders to be nothing more than an egotistical pretender whose followers had achieved very little? All that was known of Him were conflicting, unsubstantiated extraordinary tales. Nevertheless, His message continued to inspire people primarily outside Jewish societies. In light of Christianity's very slow and painful development, how can we make sense of why Christianity flourished for more than two thousand years? Perhaps it had been foretold by Isaiah. 'Yet they rebelled and grieved his Holy Spirit. So, he turned and became their enemy and he himself fought against them.'[12] Or is the answer in the Gospel itself? 'But when the Comforter is come, whom I will send unto you from the Father, even the Spirit of truth, which proceedeth from the Father, he shall testify of me: and ye also shall bear witness.'[13]

Throughout history humans seem to regularly misunderstand the words of Prophets except for those who evaluate the quality of their character attributes, something to which Jesus had referred when He said, 'Ye shall know them by their fruits.'[14] And those 'fruits' – positive attributes such as kindness, sincerity, and humility – are like signposts leading to the greatest proof of all, the Holy Spirit.

During the lives of first-generation Christians (between 26 CE and 128 CE, Christians still mainly used the Hebrew Bible as their scripture and Christianity was considered a sect within Judaism that hailed Jesus as the Messiah expected by the Jews. Even by the time the Gospel had spread through cities of the Roman Empire in the northeast corner of the Mediterranean and become established in Syria, the religion wouldn't be known as 'Christianity' and independent of Judaism until sometime in the second century CE.

The gospel of the crucifixion and resurrection was fresh for first-generation disciples active in the churches. Actual and misremembered bits of Jesus' teachings flowed – some deemed authentic and orthodox and others branded as heretical – though their origin hasn't yet been verified. Some researchers suggest that the books were not finally solidified until as late as 367 CE, as it was then that Athanasius, bishop of Alexandria, specified all 27 books.

> Forasmuch as some have taken in hand to reduce into order for themselves the books termed apocryphal and to mix them up with the divinely inspired Scripture . . . it seemed good to . . . set before you the books included in the Canon, and handed down, and accredited as Divine.[15]

Anasthasius also says the heretical writings came from the Arianism sect who believed Jesus was created by God but was not equal with God.[16] It seem odd that he includes the apocryphal books which had been identified by early church fathers to be read for instruction but said that they were 'an invention of heretics'.[17]

Christians lacked legal recognition and protection and were assumed to be guilty of certain crimes as they wouldn't participate in civil administration or military defense of the empire. They were governed by their own laws, refusing to be involved with some elements of community life, such as idolatry and sacrifice to the emperor, which the state considered signs of disloyalty. The Romans felt such non-conformity with law and order needed to be punished. Yet the laws were attractive because the Christians were models of virtue, living the life they espoused, seeking to perfectly follow Jesus' teachings.[18] And the Christian promise of eternal happiness enticed Jews as did the belief that the end of the world and kingdom of heaven were at hand.[19] Still, some 30 years after Jesus' crucifixion, James, Paul and Peter were executed and Romans destroyed the mother church in Jerusalem as well as the city itself in 70 CE.

By the second century Christ's teachings had spread throughout the Mediterranean countries where church structures were forming disparately. Some structure was based on a Greek cultural pattern, where citizens debated and decided issues and avowed that Jesus had criticized disciples who jockeyed for a position of authority over others.[20] In the Greek tradition, no follower was superior to others – Christians recalled that Jesus said His spirit would lead them to all truth. Spirit was available to all and could even visit unbaptized foreigners such as a Roman soldier. Authority in matters of doctrine was vested in the whole fellowship of believers and not in just a few leaders.

Around 135 CE when the last Jewish revolt against the Romans was quelled, some Christians believed this to be God's punishment of Israel for rejecting the Messiahship of Jesus.[21] Christians who were convinced of Jesus' imminent return rid themselves of possessions, observed celibacy and detached themselves from the world.

Christianity's separation from rabbinic Judaism was a long process.[22] Church organization was influenced by Jewish, Roman and Greek cultures. Second-century Christians participated in a church government that borrowed from Jewish structures, including presbyters as the scribes, priests as preservers and interpreters of legal and ritual traditions, and bishops as the rulers, leaders and governing authority, but not the institution of rabbis. The priests received a portion of the divine spirit that had been given to Moses, which enabled them to prophesy. Deacons oversaw the ministry of food.[23] The rank and file of believers shunned titles and any form of authority except service. Jesus' disciples claimed that He had spoken to them after the resurrection, informed them of the proper meaning of scripture and authorized them to perform miracles and initiate baptism.[24] The only recorded words of Jesus that are interpreted as designating His successorship are 'And I say also unto thee, That thou art Peter, and upon this rock I will build my church; and the gates of hell shall not prevail against it.'[25] Compare the lack of any description of Peter's authority after the ascension of Jesus with the iron-clad covenant of Bahá'u'lláh whose writings delineate His successorship from the sole interpreter 'Abdu'l-Bahá to the Guardian Shoghi Effendi to the Universal House of Justice.[26]

First-century disciples Peter and Paul – later known as bishops – both traveled to Rome, the seat of the Empire, each with different opinions. And although Paul had spoken in Acts about various church offices and had written to Timothy and Titus with more details about officials such as bishops and deacons,[27] no first century documents describe how bishops, a position that was to become primary, should be selected. Most of the information about Christian orthodox scripture is presented from the standpoint of those vying for dominance in the development of the church's structure: The ones who came out on top decided which texts to include and which would be deemed heretical. Roman Christianity, which evolved into Roman Catholicism, then comprised home churches containing schools.

Struggle among competing ideas and practices raged not just over structures but also over clearly defined rules of faith. Although the selection of scripture may seem to a modern observer as having been somewhat arbitrary at times, Bahá'u'lláh, 'Abdu'l-Bahá and Shoghi Effendi have encouraged Bahá'ís to uphold the teachings of Christianity. For example, Shoghi Effendi said, 'Peter is recognized as one whom God has caused "the mysteries of wisdom and of utterance to flow out of his mouth".'[28] 'Abdu'l-Bahá commented on the character traits of two of the disciples: 'One's conduct must be like the conduct of Paul, and one's faith similar to that of Peter.'[29]

Still, the disorganized way in which the church doctrine and authority became set contrasts starkly with the clarity of the Bahá'í Administrative Order. Shoghi Effendi laments the shakiness of the church's foundation from its beginning:

> . . . the fundamental reason why the unity of the Church of Christ was irretrievably shattered, and its influence was in the course of time undermined, was that the Edifice which the Fathers of the Church reared after the passing of His

First Apostle was an Edifice that rested in nowise upon the explicit directions of Christ Himself.[30]

The second century was the most formative one for Christianity and the big question was that of authorized scripture. Early Christians relied on the Hebrew Bible.[31] The Syrian Didache that circulated between the years 60 and 150 CE spoke of wandering prophets who carried purported sayings of Jesus.[32] 'We can surmise that the Hellenized Jewish Christians in the Didache community knew that they were living in perilous times.'[33] On the other hand, Ignatius wrote letters to Eastern churches supporting the idea of strong bishop leaders. By the end of the second century, almost all churches were governed by bishops known as Patriarchs.[34]

Although second-century Christians began seeing themselves as a third path between paganism and Judaism, they separated themselves from society and weren't concerned with sharing their message.[35] They affirmed that there was 'one God', which derived from their Jewish heritage, as well as the deity of Christ, which was connected with their own notions of salvation. Various ideas about the nature of Christ were circulating: Jesus as God; Jesus as a good man whom God adopted as His son; or the preferred concept of the oneness of God, the deity of Christ and the distinction of the Son from the Father.

Second century CE Christianity also taught that one had a choice between a materialistic life dominated by luxury, self-indulgence and shallow thoughts, or a thoughtful disciplined philosophic life. To choose the latter was also considered a conversion, literally a turning around of the soul from this changing world, but could become mainstream when the world could bear to contemplate reality and the supreme Good.[36] Most of what we know as the New Testament emerged after the second century CE, by which time the Roman church was the strongest and most influential.

As happens with in-group identity, Christian identity as a separate religion also responded to outside pressures. To the Graeco-Roman world, Christians were a sect within Judaism, whereas Jews were an established nation. Thus Roman officials treated the church as part of Judaism and didn't intrude into a Jew versus Christian argument. As the written gospels slowly emerged, Christians were seen as 'turning the world upside down' by 'upsetting traditional and accepted patterns of religious allegiance and practice'.[37] Such disruption of the social order invited punishment, which the empire didn't hesitate to bestow. For example, a pagan was forced to commit suicide under Nero for refusing to take the annual solemn oath of loyalty to the emperor, not offering sacrifice for the emperor's safety, and not believing in the divinity of the emperor's wife or the deeds of the deified Augustus and Julius. Christians inherited this legacy as they too could not accept the gods or the rites of the Graeco-Roman world. They excluded themselves from the state religion, the membership of which was considered both a social duty and an inherited practice tied to national identity. This presented society with two opposite ways of recognizing religion – either as tradition or as prophetic – affording them the choice of either adhering to the cultural and creedal status quo which is adhesion, or rejecting it, which is conversion and meant being consciously aware that one was making a considerable change by reorienting their soul. Greek philosophers' ideas, which Tatian believed were plagiarized from Moses, dominated the spiritual and intellectual life of educated people. Ironically, if this is so, the philosophers were doing a service by spreading divine teachings to counteract the pagan belief in multiple gods. The debate about what to include in the Canon stretched into the fourth century CE.[38]

Different streams of Christianity existed in the second century.[39] Christians such as Paul wanted to know who their sages and interpreters were.[40] Chroniclers circulated teachings in the second century which would later be judged as either orthodox or heretical, the latter being largely based on Gnostic ideas.

The writings of second century chroniclers Justin Martyr and Tatian – both later deemed heretics – provide a fuller picture of those times. The former said he'd been attracted to Christianity by how Christians behaved in the face of death. In his search for truth, the pagan Tatian was attracted to the idea in Jewish scripture of a single ruler of the universe[41] as well as the distinction made between God and Logos (the Word) with God working through Logos.

The Baháʼí writings delve deeply into the meaning of the Word:

> Now, if we were to understand manifestational procession as 'appearance' rather than 'division into parts', we have already stated that this is the manner of the procession and appearance of the Holy Spirit and the Word, which are from God. As it is said in the Gospel of John, 'In the beginning was the Word, and the Word was with God.'[42] It follows then that the Holy Spirit and the Word are the appearance of God and consist in the divine perfections that shone forth in the reality of Christ . . . The perfections of Christ are called the Word since all created things are like individual letters, and individual letters do not convey a complete meaning, while the perfections of Christ are even as an entire word, for from a word a complete meaning can be inferred . . . And know that the procession of the Word and the Holy Spirit from God, which is a manifestational procession and appearance, should not be taken to mean that the reality of the Divinity has been divided or multiplied, or has descended from its heights of purity and sanctity. God forbid! . . . If a clear and spotless mirror were placed before the sun, the light and heat, the form and image of the sun would appear therein with such a manifestational appearance that if a beholder were to say, 'This is the sun', he would be speaking the truth. But the mirror is the mirror and the sun is the sun. The sun is but one sun, and remains one even if it appears in numerous mirrors.[43]

Tatian was also influenced by Greek myths about God incarnating into human form,[44] a belief that has survived in many Christian denominations. He asked questions that aren't often asked these days, such as, what does the Genesis verse mean when it states that man was created in God's image? And what is the notion of the Fall? He maintained the logical supposition that after the Fall, man didn't lose free will but retained it. And although the 'first man' had freely chosen to follow the arch-rebel, humanity can redeem itself via the knowledge of God.⁴⁵ He also said that body and soul aren't enough: 'Without the spirit, man is superior to animals only in his articulate speech'⁴⁶ and that 'soul and spirit can unite by way of the knowledge of God'.⁴⁷ Greek philosopher Diogenes used the analogy of the soul's relation to the body to illustrate that the Christian faith provided spiritual insight and moral virtue for society.

Bible scholar Bart Ehrman says,

> . . . variant readings should not be discarded as trivial and useless as we forge backward to the original text. The variants themselves can be of supreme importance for certain kinds of questions, not questions about what an author wrote but about what scribes may have wanted him to say.⁴⁸

I present these ideas to show how they may seem reasonable rather than heretical to a modern person, and also not as improbable as a doctrine that upholds the idea of a bodily resurrection. Thus from the standpoint of the 21st century, the charge of heresy against these early writers seems exaggerated or worse. Fortunately, Bahá'ís have Bahá'u'lláh's Kitáb-i-Íqán that explains how to understand symbolic language in words used by the Manifestations. The Bahá'í Faith also has 'Abdu'l-Bahá, appointed by Bahá'u'lláh to be the interpreter of His teachings,⁴⁹ who clearly explains scripture in simple terms, and Shoghi Effendi, 'the expounder of the words of God'.⁵⁰

Similar to the difficulties experienced by Christians in becoming recognized as an independent religion, the Bábís and later the Bahá'ís, particularly in Islamic countries were met with charges of being against the established order. One of Shoghi Effendi's earliest tasks was to work to obtain official state recognition for the Bahá'í Faith through the legal incorporation of its institutions,⁵¹ and particularly in predominantly Islamic countries, such as Egypt.⁵²

Second century Christians clearly thought they possessed an understanding greater than any other belief in the classical world. But they needed to come to terms with the idea that their internal disagreements were based mainly on their cultural ideology that fused together religion and politics. An inability to separate cultural values and personal ideas from the teachings of a Manifestation is a frequent theme throughout the Baháʼí writings, such as when Baháʼu'lláh calls out humanity for being attached to idle fancies and vain imaginings. When Christians converted from paganism, it meant leaving an identity of 'persons of Graeco-Roman culture' who weren't just changing their behavior but following their own individual conscience.[53]

At the end of the second Christian century, Bishop Irenaeus had helped establish the four-gospel canon, and ensured that the teachings of Paul and John weren't overshadowed by Gnostic sects. Controversies in the second-century church included a Gnostic idea that the material world is evil as well as a Gnostic belief that there could be no resurrection of the body because the spirit alone is capable of salvation. A more problematic Gnostic belief was that moral conduct may be ascetic or licentious, depending on whether one denied and disciplined his body or indulged it. Another Gnostic belief more consistent with other religious scriptures was that reason is part of human nature but can become distinct in the spoken word, so Christ could be seen as divine but distinct from God.

Because Baháʼís can refer to written texts containing the words of the Báb and Baháʼu'lláh and interpreted by ʻAbdu'l-Bahá and Shoghi Effendi, we can study and meditate on the precise creative word. But with only second-hand sources such as Christians had, it had to have been much more difficult.

2
First Century American Bahá'ís

It might seem fanciful for a historical account to mention the workings of spirit in the unfolding of human events. And yet I didn't understand history until I encountered the idea of progressive revelation, with the rise and fall of human societies according to the cycle of divine revelations. A late Bahá'í friend of mine used to say that as an art history major in the 1960s, she made the connection between new types of architecture arising just after the establishment of a new world religion. That is, she noticed how in past centuries architectural design changed dramatically – such as between churches and mosques, for example – with the appearance of new religions. But she was confused about new trends in art and architecture in the 19th century, which led her on a search until she found the Bahá'í Faith. She had figured that new Revelations released spiritual powers. We don't yet have language to specify what it means to say 'spiritual powers were released' but the Bahá'í writings frequently mention this reality.

Thus we see two Manifestations of God appear in the mid-19th century in a country that had sunk so low from the pinnacle of Islamic culture that its political and spiritual leaders would falsely accuse and condemn to death innocents just to steal their fortunes. And the United States, which viewed itself as a great and unique experiment in democracy and freedom, was denying its genocide of the indigenous inhabitants of the American continent and the enslavement of Africans. Indeed, even now in the 21st century, teaching school children about the treatment by the United States of its conquered and enslaved minorities is being legislated against in some states.

Shoghi Effendi doesn't mince his words about the times we're still living in:

> A tempest, unprecedented in its violence, unpredictable in its course, catastrophic in its immediate effects, unimaginably glorious in its ultimate consequences, is at present sweeping the face of the earth. Its driving power is remorselessly gaining in range and momentum. Its cleansing force, however much undetected, is increasing with every passing day. Humanity, gripped in the clutches of its devastating power, is smitten by the evidences of its resistless fury. It can neither perceive its origin, nor probe its significance, nor discern its outcome. Bewildered, agonized and helpless, it watches this great and mighty wind of God invading the remotest and fairest regions of the earth, rocking its foundations, deranging its equilibrium, sundering its nations, disrupting the homes of its peoples, wasting its cities, driving into exile its kings, pulling down its bulwarks, uprooting its institutions, dimming its light, and harrowing up the souls of its inhabitants.
>
> 'The time for the destruction of the world and its people', Bahá'u'lláh's prophetic pen has proclaimed, 'hath arrived.'[1]

Forty-nine years after the Báb declared to Mullá Ḥusayn that He was the present-day Promised One, the words of Bahá'u'lláh – the subsequent Promised One – were quoted on the American continent. The occasion was the 1893 World's Parliament of Religions during the Columbian Exposition in Chicago, Illinois, a year after Bahá'u'lláh's ascension. The quote, read by Rev. Henry Jessup, who was visiting from Syria, were words recorded by Edward Granville Browne three years previously which, Jessup said, 'gave utterance to sentiments so noble, so Christlike, that we repeat them as our closing words':

> That all nations should become one in faith and all men as brothers; that the bonds of affection and unity between the sons of men should be strengthened; that diversity of

religions should cease and differences of race be annulled. What harm is there in this? Yet so it shall be. These fruitless strifes, these ruinous wars shall pass away, and the 'Most Great Peace' shall come. Do not you in Europe need this also? Let not a man glory in this, that he loves his country; let him rather glory in this, that he loves his kind.[2]

We're told that there's a power in the words of Manifestations. That power was released that day.

Information about Bahá'u'lláh's Cause soon became available to Americans through Ibrahim Kheiralla,[3] a businessman from Syria who spoke English and knew something about the Bahá'í Faith, inaccurate though it was. Kheiralla had learned about the Bahá'í Faith from 'Abdu'l-Karím Ṭihrání whom he met in Egypt, among other Persian exiles. Ṭihrání also urged him to abandon his interest in black magic.[4] Kheiralla had heard about Bahá'u'lláh and sent Him a letter telling of his acceptance, as there was no official method of enrolling in the Faith at that time. Bahá'u'lláh replied, encouraging him to hold fast to 'that which will draw you nearer to God'.[5]

As Kheiralla was finalizing his plans to travel to the United States in May 1892, he heard of Bahá'u'lláh's passing.[6] The only teachings he learned had been shared with him over the course of two years by an early Bahá'í in Egypt via imperfect oral translations.[7] This may have been supplemented by the many stories about Bahá'u'lláh told during his study in Cairo.[8]

From his western-style evangelical education, Kheiralla had learned that everyone is capable of reading the Bible and independently determining its truth. What distinguished him from other Middle Eastern Christians was his sense of autonomy in interpreting texts as opposed to seeking out clergy for scriptural guidance. Apparently, he transferred this training to his teaching of the Bahá'í Faith, although he wrote that the only words of Bahá'u'lláh he knew 'were those which I [later] read in the books of Prof. E. G. Browne, of Cambridge, England, and a few communes and tablets which I had copied in Cairo, Egypt, before I came to America'.[9]

Within a few years Kheiralla, using mainly biblical prophecies, was sharing his understanding of the Baháʼí teachings with a growing audience of mostly Protestant Christians. Though he could impart only a few words of Baháʼuʼlláh in his spiritual classes, he also included a great deal of inaccurate information. Yet he still attracted believers. Compare this situation with the confusion during Christianity in its second century when there was no way to access scripture recorded directly from Jesus' words.

Kheiralla's business partner went to America to try to sell one of Kheiralla's inventions, a ticket with space for advertising, with Kheiralla following some time later.[10] When this and other ventures failed, Kheiralla found other ways to support himself and his family in Egypt. Settling in Chicago, he set up a healing practice, advertising his self-perceived supernatural powers of healing. While treating his patients, he would tell them about Baháʼuʼlláh, embellished with his own personal interpretations.[11]

Soon Kheiralla was conducting 13-part classes on the nature of the mind and the needs of the soul. He included a discussion about the importance of prayer, handing out copies of Baháʼuʼlláh's prayers without divulging the source.[12] In the final three classes[13] of each session, he presented the Faith, Baháʼuʼlláh and ʻAbduʼl-Bahá through a prophetic Christian lens, claiming that Baháʼuʼlláh was God and ʻAbduʼl-Bahá the return of Jesus Christ.[14] In those days, people who were also attracted by alternatives to traditional religions often sought out healing philosophies. Such people gravitated to each other and shared their information, thus creating a network where new ideas, like the Baháʼí Faith, could spread.[15]

One individual who was drawn to the Faith was Phoebe Hearst, wife of a wealthy businessman turned Senator. Introduced to the religion by Edward and Lua Getsinger, this woman of means wanted to organize what became the first American pilgrimage to ʻAkká to meet ʻAbduʼl-Bahá.[16] The pilgrims brought along a manuscript about the Faith that Kheiralla hoped to publish and learned that it included much erroneous information, such as reincarnation and occultism. The

pilgrims returned home, enlightened by teachings direct from
'Abdu'l-Bahá with whom they remained in constant communication, frequently writing to Him with questions. Meanwhile,
Kheiralla's sense of self-importance as the main Bahá'í teacher
in America had even led him to tell a *New York Herald* reporter
that he was the 'center' of the Bahá'í Faith in America.[17] He also
openly criticized other prominent Bahá'í teachers.

Even after cautionary warnings, Kheiralla continued to
spread his alternative theories throughout the United States,
causing 'Abdu'l-Bahá to dispatch a Persian Bahá'í, 'Abdu'l-Karím
Ṭihrání, to investigate things, to help Kheiralla back into the
Faith and to educate the Bahá'ís about its true teachings.[18]

Still, Kheiralla felt that his success in attracting believers to the
Bahá'í Faith should allow him to be promoted to an imagined
higher station and he sent a letter in 1900 to 'Abdu'l-Bahá suggesting as much. 'Abdu'l-Bahá replied that no Bahá'í would be
promoted to any station whatsoever since the Faith doesn't allow
clergy. This resulted in Kheiralla editing his manuscript by replacing all mention of 'Abdu'l-Bahá with allusions to Bahá'u'lláh's
other sons and daughters. The unfortunate result was that the
friction ignited by Kheiralla threatened the unity of the fledgling
American Bahá'í community. Even as these issues worked themselves out, by 1899 membership had grown to nearly 1500.[19]

About the early believers, the book *Century of Light* records:

> Their response arose from a level of consciousness that recognized, even if sometimes only dimly, the desperate need
> of the human race for spiritual enlightenment. To remain
> steadfast in their commitment to this insight required of
> these early believers – on whose sacrifice of self much of
> the foundation of the present-day Bahá'í communities both
> in the West and many other lands were laid – that they
> resist not only family and social pressures, but also the easy
> rationalizations of the world-view in which they had been
> raised and to which everything around them insistently
> exposed them. There was a heroism about the steadfastness
> of these early Western Bahá'ís that is, in its own way, as

affecting as that of their Persian co-religionists who, in these same years, were facing persecution and death for the Faith they had embraced.[20]

'Abdu'l-Bahá wrote to the American community that when they were united, He would come for a visit, which He did in 1912.[21] Besides desiring to visit a unified Bahá'í community, He also saw this trip as an opportunity to warn America and Europe to try to halt the machinery leading to an impending world war, whose signs He had read clearly. To that end, He had been in correspondence with the secretary of the Lake Mohonk Conference on International Arbitration since August 1911 and it was that organization that issued the first invitation and persuaded Him to travel to the US. The Bahá'ís arranged invitations for Him, not just on peace but on many topics, including racism, women's equality, science and religion, politics, the oneness of humanity and the nature of religion. He traveled coast to coast speaking to hundreds of audiences. But the world clung to its 19th century thinking as royalty butted heads over which branches of their extended families would rule over which territories.

'Abdu'l-Bahá also made sure that news reporters understood His mission for peace. In the more than 40 cities He visited, He spent time meeting with, teaching and encouraging the Bahá'ís. Unfortunately, the US population continued to choose to follow leaders who had launched the first organized government-sponsored propaganda campaign in the country headed up by the Committee for Public Information.[22] Their work leading up to the first World War several years later convinced a previously anti-war population of US families to send their sons to battle, ignoring 'Abdu'l-Bahá's message of peace. American individuals thus had been persuaded by national myths and chose instead their leaders' rhetoric rather than 'to see with his own eyes and hear with his own ears'.[23] During the one-hundred-plus years that have passed since then, the population has tolerated, if not supported and paid for, a nearly continuous armed combat around the globe.

The United States didn't suffer the physical destruction of World War One, though veterans, families and citizens experienced trauma. Even as the weary soldiers, who managed not to be turned into fodder, limped back home, the Versailles agreement left Germany feeling like a helpless victim, licking its wounds until it would emerge again, stronger and ready to wreak more havoc before 20 years had passed.

While opinion leaders weren't ready to give up their 19th-century consciousness, others hungered for peace and wanted it to spread. The Baháʼí Faith experienced a new stage in its growth in the United States after ʻAbdu'l-Baháʼs visit. He had energized His followers and attracted more souls to His cause.

Shoghi Effendi was studying at Oxford University in 1921 when he received the shocking news that his beloved grandfather, ʻAbdu'l-Bahá, had passed away. He was devastated by the passing of his grandfather. In an undated letter written to a Baháʼí student in London, Shoghi Effendi said, 'The stir which is now aroused in the Baháʼí world is an impetus to the Cause and will awaken every faithful soul to shoulder the responsibilities which the Master has now placed on every one of us.' In the letter he made reference to his imminent departure for Haifa.[24]

Soon after his arrival, ʻAbdu'l-Baháʼs Will was read and Shoghi Effendi was stunned when he learned of his appointment as Guardian of the Baháʼí Faith.[25]

Shoghi Effendi spent the next four decades 'erecting, on the foundation created by the Master, an organized system',[26] directing the Baháʼís how to function in an administrative order and increasing the reach of the religion to the entire planet. He translated major works and passages from the writings which helped him interpret such procedures as establishing and giving to funds, holding elections and the functioning of elected bodies. His widow, Rúhíyyih Khánum, worried about the pressure and stress that befell him.

> I am really worried over Shoghi Effendi. When he used to get so very distressed and upset in the past it affected him, but not as it does now. Sometimes I think it will lead to

his premature death . . . he breathes so hard, almost like one who has been running, and he has such huge shadows under his eyes. He forces himself to go on and finish the letters he has had piled for days on his desk – but he reads a thing sometimes ten minutes over and over because he can't concentrate![27]

After his death she wrote,

The degree to which Shoghi Effendi sacrificed himself in every human sense is unbelievable – he had no life of his own, no time of his own, practically no joys of his own, very little happiness in all of his life.[28]

In the days of letter-writing and telegrams, Shoghi Effendi kept in touch with Bahá'í communities and individuals wherever they were. On the brink of the next world war, he wrote to the Bahá'ís of the United States and Canada:

The one chief remaining citadel, the mighty arm which still raises aloft the standard of an unconquerable Faith, is none other than the blessed community of the followers of the Most Great Name in the North American continent.[29]

He pressed this point:

The glowing tributes . . . paid to the capacity, the spirit, the conduct, and the high rank, of the American believers . . . must, under no circumstances, be confounded with the characteristics and nature of the people from which God has raised them up. A sharp distinction between that community and that people must be made and reasonably and fearlessly upheld, if we wish to give due recognition to the transmuting power of the Faith of Bahá'u'lláh in its impact on the lives and standards of those who have chosen to enlist under His banner.[30]

FIRST CENTURY AMERICAN BAHÁ'ÍS

One of the biggest obstacles to the acceptance of Bahá'u'lláh's revelation has been what Shoghi Effendi referred to as 'spiritual degeneration' with materialism as its offspring in the mid-20th century.

> As outside forces manipulated new governments, attention was increasingly diverted from an objective consideration of developmental needs to ideological and political struggles that bore little or no relation to social or economic reality. The results were uniformly devastating.[31]

Century of Light contrasts an orientation towards materialism with that towards spirituality and says that predicting the outcomes of these opposite orientations is 'simplicity itself':

> Reality – including human reality and the process by which it evolves – is essentially material in nature. The goal of human life is, or ought to be, the satisfaction of material needs and wants. Society exists to facilitate this quest, and the collective concern of humankind should be an ongoing refinement of the system, aimed at rendering it ever more efficient in carrying out its assigned task.[32]

A curious measure of the value system on planet Earth can be found in the popular weekly *Time* magazine which annually designates a 'person of the year'. Their selection seems to be inspired by the 'Great Man Theory' of history, which asserts that individuals have power to transform society. The selections are typically males with a notable measure of monetary or political power, attributes most prized by American culture which has been increasingly steeped in materialism. How unfortunate that *Time* in the first half of the 20th century never identified Shoghi Effendi's cogent diagnosis of a spiritual degeneration as the root of the problems besetting the world.

As *Century of Light* further notes:

Inspiring these political, social and economic crises was the inexorable rise and consolidation of a disease of the human soul infinitely more destructive than any of its specific manifestations. Its triumph marked a new and ominous stage in the process of social and spiritual degeneration that Shoghi Effendi had identified. Fathered by nineteenth century European thought, acquiring enormous influence through the achievements of American capitalist culture, and endowed by Marxism with the counterfeit credibility peculiar to that system, materialism emerged full-blown in the second half of the twentieth century as a kind of universal religion claiming absolute authority in both the personal and social life of humankind. Its creed was simplicity itself.[33]

There were a few glimmers of higher ethical standards. After the stock market crash in 1929, which led to the Great Depression, until 1941 the federal government created work relief programs to assist the poor and the elderly. Moreover, some veterans of the second World War, having experienced foreign cultures, people, cuisines, as well as interracial interactions and friendships, returned home to the US with a greater awareness of people from other cultures.

The world shrank even more as nations connected via television broadcasts and more people had grown used to the idea of air travel. Decades of war had ravaged much of the world's economies but the economy in the US, whose territory had escaped the wars unscathed, boomed as the country helped devastated Europe and Japan recover. As well, major US corporations had profited from subsidiaries in Nazi Germany, even going so far as to save costs and increase profits by relying on slave labor performed by Jews and prisoners of war.[34] Whereas before the war the United States had been primarily agricultural, it emerged from World War Two as the world's strongest military power.[35] Arms dealers continued to capitalize on fear and found opportunities in the Far East to peddle their wares, particularly from dread of the power of totalitarian countries like the USSR that sought to spread its communist system.

As Shoghi Effendi had prophetically warned, forces undermining inherited systems and convictions of every kind were continuing to advance in tandem with the integrating processes at work in the world. It is not surprising, therefore, that the euphoria induced by the restoration of peace in both Europe and the Orient proved to be of the briefest duration. Hardly had hostilities ended than the ideological divisions between Marxism and liberal democracy burst out into attempts to secure dominance between the respective blocs of nations they inspired. The phenomenon of 'Cold War', in which the struggle for advantage stopped just short of military conflict, emerged as the prevailing political paradigm of the next several decades.[36]

At the same time, the fruits of this prosperity – suburban houses, new cars and other consumer goods – were available to more US citizens than ever before. Babies born just after the war and who came of age in the 1960s would grow up amid increased prosperity in the country. After the two wars, the great depression and the economic boom of the 1950s, a more optimistic mood prevailed.

However, the 1950s also saw great conflict domestically. A nascent civil rights movement emerged in America when there was uproar at the racism that welcomed home African American veterans, who had served their country bravely, by restricting their access to the same benefits given to their white brothers-in-arms.

Further, the crusade against communism abroad, this time leading to the Korean War, also exposed underlying divisions in American society. Youth were protesting the continuous wars as well as participating in growing movements for the equality for women and minorities and environmental awareness. An often overlooked detail is how the 'beat' generation, many of whom had grown up in families whose fathers were fighting in Europe, were inspired to explore the spirituality of eastern religions, specifically Buddhism, as they proposed a 'revolt of the soul'.[37] To others these religions seemed somewhat sinister;

for example, FBI director J. Edgar Hoover saw them as enemies on a par with communists and intellectuals, as he stated at the 1960 Republican National Convention.[38] With such branding, it's fair to say that some Christian Americans were wary of any foreign-sounding religions.

There was also a great deal of movement in the development of the Bahá'í Faith in this period. The Guardian thoroughly studied the writings of his great-grandfather Bahá'u'lláh and his grandfather 'Abdu'l-Bahá, who had both initiated the way, in place of a clergy, the Bahá'í Cause would govern itself. As soon as he took up his role as Guardian, Shoghi Effendi methodically, systematically, meticulously began building the worldwide administrative order outlined in the writings of Bahá'u'lláh and 'Abdu'l-Bahá, whose progress he communicated in letters sent to National Assemblies who passed them along to communities so they could be read at Nineteen Day Feasts throughout the world as the religion spread. The foundation of this Administrative Order comprised assemblies of nine members elected in localities according to their civic jurisdictions, whether it be villages, cities, counties, townships or other configurations, depending on how jurisdictions were organized in different places. In 1953 he launched a Plan to extend this work. This plan differed from the first and second Seven Year Plans of the North American community inasmuch as its scope was worldwide.

Those who heeded his call to leave their homes and become the first Bahá'ís to live in a particular country he titled Knights of Bahá'u'lláh. The overall objective of the Ten Year Plan was to 'open' a significant number of countries to the Bahá'í Faith and to bring people into the religion. When there were enough Bahá'ís in one locality, a local spiritual assembly could be established, thereby more fully developing the Administrative Order. Once enough local spiritual assemblies had been established in a country, a national spiritual assembly could be elected. When there were enough national spiritual assemblies in the world, their members would elect the Universal House of Justice. To assist in this process, Shoghi Effendi appointed sincere, dedicated helpers as Hands of the Cause of God, whom he designated 'Chief Stewards of Bahá'u'lláh's embryonic World Commonwealth... with the dual function of guarding over the security, and of insuring the propagation, of the Bahá'í Faith'.[39]

One of the goals of the Plan was to quadruple the number of national spiritual assemblies.[40] Shoghi Effendi stressed the point he'd made about the character of the nations that were singled out for such tasks:

> How often have the Prophets of God, not excepting Bahá'u'lláh Himself, chosen to appear, and deliver their Message in countries and amidst peoples and races, at a time when they were either fast declining, or had already touched the lowest depths of moral and spiritual degradation.[41]

In the United States, despite the nation's tolerance for war and glorification of the military, the Bahá'í Faith and its message of peace spread, largely by the efforts of a few stalwarts working quietly and tirelessly, attracting waiting souls, helping them explore the reality of their true spiritual nature, and enabling them to contribute to the worldwide effort of developing the Administrative Order, a major component of the 'ever-advancing civilization' which Bahá'u'lláh said all people had been 'created to carry forward'.[42]

Election of the Universal House of Justice

The Guardian created the International Bahá'í Council in 1951, identifying it as a forerunner to the Universal House of Justice.[43] He knew that a world body needed a firm foundation for stability, thus he planned to establish enough local spiritual assemblies in a number of nations on each continent to support a national spiritual assembly in each country, which in turn would serve as a strong pillar of the Universal House of Justice. His Ten Year Plan unfolded in stages, the first involving as many as possible of 131 territories where there were no

Bahá'ís,[44] and later forming 15 national assemblies. By the end of the Plan, Bahá'ís were residing in 4,500 localities worldwide[45] where they consolidated their communities as well as opened new territories on all continents and islands. The Plan spelled out certain principles for national assemblies to encourage and guide them, such as to regard their work as the 'healthy heart in the community, pumping spiritual love [and] energy', to 'regard itself as a loving parent', and to 'avoid adding rules and regulations of procedure'. Shoghi Effendi sought to increase the number of representatives from minority peoples in the Faith and the number of localities where Bahá'ís resided, as well as the number of local assemblies and the number of incorporated assemblies. He also urged believers to use summer schools as venues for learning, making friends and increasing unity and love. And he warned that 'the path ahead is thorny and tortuous, with tests and trials abounding'.[46]

Tragically, Shoghi Effendi passed away in 1957, so his Plans ended with the close of the Ten Year Crusade in 1963. Because he hadn't left a Will, had had no children and the Aghṣán relatives had challenged and broken Bahá'u'lláh's covenant by denying the authority of 'Abdu'l-Bahá and Shoghi Effendi, the Hands faced a reality not explicitly covered in any of the writings. Stunned, grieving and aware that they had no legislative authority, they were uncertain about whether there was guidance about appointing another Guardian. Having gathered in London for Shoghi Effendi's funeral, the Hands 'decided not an instant's time must be lost in holding a plenary meeting' of all of them at the World Centre, which they scheduled for 18 November 1957. Their 'first act was to choose a delegation to open the apartment of Shoghi Effendi, which had been sealed by the International Bahá'í Council right after his passing . . . and to make an exhaustive search for any document he might have left – a Will or otherwise. There was no such thing to be found.'[47]

After his passing, the Hands – the Custodians of the Bahá'í Faith who had been appointed by Shoghi Effendi – met to 'ensure that everything connected with the affairs, direction and administration of the Faith was solidly and speedily vested in the Institution of the Hands'.[48] They issued a number of formal statements and unanimous proclamations to the community regarding their responsibility to 'preserve the unity, the security and the development of the Bahá'í World Community and all its institutions'.[49] They also settled on a mode of operation.[50] Further, they were able to secure the legal right to the Shrines and properties as well as the right to direct the affairs of the Cause,[51] on the strength of the statement in the last letter of Shoghi Effendi, written in October 1957, designating the Hands of the Cause as the 'Chief Stewards of Bahá'u'lláh's embryonic World Commonwealth, who have been invested by the unerring Pen of the Center of His Covenant with the dual function of guarding over the security, and of insuring the propagation, of His Father's Faith'.[52]

On 4 November 1959 they informed the worldwide Bahá'í membership of their plans, which included the election in 1961 of the International Bahá'í Council, previously an appointed body, for a two-year term, to culminate with the election of the Universal House of Justice in 1963. Their message included the words of Shoghi Effendi:

> 'When that divinely-ordained Body comes into existence, all the conditions of the Faith can be examined anew and the measures necessary for its future operation determined in consultation with the Hands of the Cause.' This includes the subject of the Guardianship.[53]

The Hands understood that only the Universal House of Justice would be able to determine the question of the guardianship and that it could not be established until there were an adequate number of national assemblies. The Guardian often compared national assemblies with pillars supporting the dome, which is the Universal House of Justice, the national assemblies themselves resting upon the local assemblies and the work of individual believers who are like the foundational building blocks. By the end of the Ten Year Crusade 1963 there were 306 local spiritual assemblies, 682 groups comprising between two and eight adults, 714 locations where isolated Baháʼís lived[54] and 56 national spiritual assemblies established, surpassing the goal of 48.

Only one man among the ranks of the 27 living Hands fomented disunity when he declared himself the next Guardian and created an uproar in the Baháʼí community. In a remarkable, unprecedented, selfless and noble manner, the rest of the Hands reminded the worldwide Baháʼí community that Mr Remey did not fulfill any of the qualifications for guardianship set out in the Will and Testament of ʻAbduʼl‑Bahá.[55] Sharply contrasting Remey's self-proclamation, the Hands even determined that they themselves should not be considered for election to the Universal House of Justice.[56]

> Never before had persons into whose hands the supreme power in a great religion had fallen and who enjoyed a level of regard unmatched by any others in the community, required not to be considered for participation in the exercise of supreme authority, placing themselves entirely at the service of the Body chosen by the community of their fellow believers for this role.[57]

Years before, Shoghi Effendi described the negative forces prevalent in the world into which the Universal House of Justice was born:

> The Spirit that has incarnated itself in the institutions of a rising Faith has, in the course of its onward march for the redemption of the world, encountered and is now battling with such forces as are, in most instances, the very negation of that Spirit, and whose continued existence must inevitably hinder it from achieving its purpose. The hollow and outworn institutions, the obsolescent doctrines and beliefs, the effete and discredited traditions, which these forces represent, it should be observed, have in certain instances been undermined by virtue of their senility, the loss of their cohesive power, and their own inherent corruption.[58]

When this passage was written, one world war had just finished, an economic depression was devastating much of the world and another war was in the making. The Faith itself was constantly beset with troubles that threatened to destroy it. Bahá'ís of those times had difficulty imagining that a House of Justice would be established in their lifetime. However, Shoghi Effendi filtered world events through a spiritual lens, laying out an optimistic future designed by Bahá'u'lláh's revelation.

> A twofold process, however, can be distinguished, each tending, in its own way and with an accelerated momentum, to bring to a climax the forces that are transforming the face of our planet. The first is essentially an integrating process, while the second is fundamentally disruptive. The former, as it steadily evolves, unfolds a System which may well serve as a pattern for that world polity towards which a strangely disordered world is continually advancing; while the latter, as its disintegrating influence deepens, tends to tear down, with increasing violence, the antiquated barriers that seek to block humanity's progress towards its destined goal. The constructive process stands associated with the nascent Faith of Bahá'u'lláh, and is the harbinger of the New World Order that Faith must erelong establish. The destructive forces that characterize the other should be identified with a civilization that has refused to answer to the expectation of a new age, and is consequently falling into chaos and decline.[59]

As the Hands translated Shoghi Effendi's vision into reality, they continued to engage in the work of helping to reconstruct a crumbling world social system. Thus, with national spiritual assemblies having been established in all corners of the world, they made preparations for all the national assembly members to meet at the Bahá'í World Centre in Haifa to elect the first Universal House of Justice during the Festival of Riḍván in April 1963.

The Nine Year Plan

The new House of Justice wrote:

> The Ten Year Crusade . . . saw the Cause of God leap forward in one mighty decade-long effort to the point at which the foundations of its Administrative Order were laid throughout the world, thus preparing the way for that awakening of the masses which must characterize the future progress of the Faith.[60]

The Báb and Bahá'u'lláh had placed great emphasis on sharing the divine teachings. 'Abdu'l-Bahá said that He 'spent His days and nights in promoting the Cause and urging the peoples to service'.[61] Shoghi Effendi had initiated a succession of national, international and global Plans based on 'Abdu'l-Bahá's Tablets of the Divine Plan and a long succession of Plans would be launched by the Universal House of Justice extending through both the Formative and Golden Ages of the Faith.[62] The House of Justice noted that the two objectives of its first Plan were expansion and universal participation and assigned goals to the 69 national communities under the leadership of 69 national spiritual assemblies. It called upon the Hands of the Cause and their auxiliaries to continue as standard-bearers of the new Plan.[63]

In its message, the House of Justice noted that the Faith now comprised a much greater number and diversity of national communities than had existed a decade earlier, which had consisted of only 12 national communities. Each of the goal countries now had a National Spiritual Assembly. The Crusade had begun with a little more than 600 local spiritual assemblies, mostly in Persia, North America and Europe, whereas by 1964 there were close to 4,600 throughout the continents and islands of the world.[64]

3
The Sixties

A historian opens his article with this comment:

> Historians in the future may come to rank the 1960s alongside the 1520s and the 1790s among the great revolutionary decades of Europe's religious history. Indeed, the religious significance of the 1960s is even wider, since equally radical changes were taking place in North America and Australasia. And the atmosphere of the Sixties also had much in common with that of those other revolutionary decades. History moved faster during these years, and a dynamic of change built up which old institutions and traditions were powerless to withstand.[1]

The period 1964–73 in the United States is noteworthy not just from a socio-historical standpoint, but also for developments in the Bahá'í Faith. It was a period of starkly contrasting growth and destruction. The Guardian had written,

> As we view the world around us, we are compelled to observe the manifold evidences of that universal fermentation which, in every continent of the globe and in every department of human life, be it religious, social, economic or political, is purging and reshaping humanity in anticipation of the Day when the wholeness of the human race will have been recognized and its unity established. A twofold process, however, can be distinguished, each tending, in its own way and with an accelerated momentum, to bring to a climax the forces that are transforming the face of our

planet. The first is essentially an integrating process, while the second is fundamentally disruptive.[2]

Within its first year, the Universal House of Justice had crafted an ambitious Nine Year Plan. Bahá'í membership in the United States grew exponentially throughout the decade, particularly among youth who'd been looking for answers to the grave issues affecting them, especially a senseless war that was devouring young men. These youth were among the first second-century Bahá'ís.

The beginning of the second Bahá'í century coincided with the end of World War Two. The United States was positioned for phenomenal economic growth and came to be considered a military superpower. Trends emerged in the 1960s that seemed to break sharply with a more artificial and staid 1950s. New research inspired an awareness of ecology and environmental interconnectedness which led to ecological activism and an interest in organic food. A second wave in the feminist movement flourished. Material and spiritual self-healing became popular via nutritional supplements and meditation practices. The nation began to pay more attention to the increasing efforts of people of color who were organizing politically to assert their rights. The famed African American civil rights leader Dr Martin Luther King Jr in August 1963 delivered his now famous 'I Have a Dream'[3] speech in the nation's capital to an audience of pro-civil rights demonstrators. The speech, envisioning a world when black and white people would live in harmony, is now broadcast annually on a federal holiday established in King's honor, a reality that the 1960s could not have foreseen. Similarly unforeseen is the present-day annual death count of innocent African American citizens killed in cold blood, whether by armed vigilantes or armed police. The American Indian Movement took form in 1968 initially to assist indigenous people who had been displaced from their tribes to speak up for equal treatment with an ultimate goal of gaining tribal sovereignty.

In the international theater, relations between the two

superpowers were deteriorating in 1960 when the Soviets shot down an American U-2 spy plane deep inside their territory. Yet, as if in counterpoint, the youthful president John F. Kennedy, who took office in January 1961 – the first Catholic to be elected president – brought an energy that inspired young people. He pronounced in his inaugural address, 'Ask not what your country can do for you – ask what you can do for your country,'[4] challenging citizens to contribute to the public good; he declared a technological race into outer space – dubbed a space race – against the US nemesis and sworn enemy the Soviet Union. This inspired schools to focus on science education and afforded youth an inspirational vision. He also created the Peace Corps in 1961, spurring young people to volunteer to serve as peace ambassadors and volunteer development workers in other countries, a counterbalance to serving in the military.

Meanwhile the policies of Soviet Premier Khrushchev were focused on spreading Communism, which was a constant worry for the United States. He agreed to the construction of the Berlin Wall to stop East Germans from escaping to West Germany.[5] A big worry for the United States was that Cuba, only 103 miles from the Florida coast, had turned socialist in 1959, nationalizing all foreign assets and creating a trade relationship with the USSR, prompting the US to impose a trade embargo and to cut diplomatic ties. The US implemented a plan of the previous administration to try to overthrow Castro. This 'Bay of Pigs invasion' failed.

Further, 'shortly after the Berlin wall was erected, a standoff between U.S. and Soviet troops on either side of the diplomatic checkpoint led to one of the tensest moments of the Cold War in Europe'.[6] An additional 1,500 American soldiers arrived in West Berlin. Then, in response to moves by the Soviet Union to cut off all access to Berlin, President Kennedy ordered 148,000 Guardsmen and Reservists to active duty, my father among them.

Tensions mounted even higher the following autumn when the United States discovered Soviet nuclear missiles stationed in Cuba and braced itself for nuclear conflict, but after a standoff,

Khrushchev agreed to remove the weapons on condition the US agreed not to invade Cuba and to remove its missiles from Turkey.[7]

Kennedy's assassination in November 1963 killed the faint promise of peace. *Century of Light* sums up the world political situation in the 20th century:

> As outside forces manipulated new governments, attention was increasingly diverted from an objective consideration of developmental needs to ideological and political struggles that bore little or no relation to social or economic reality. The results were uniformly devastating. Economic bankruptcy, gross violations of human rights, the breakdown of civil administration and the rise of opportunistic elites who saw in the suffering of their countries only openings for self-enrichment – such was the heartbreaking fate that engulfed one after another of the new nations who, only short years before, had begun life with such great promise.[8]

Even as the country still reeled from Kennedy's tragic assassination, less than a year later it fully engaged in a war triggered by an actual or perceived Vietnamese attack on an American ship in the Gulf of Tonkin, Vietnam, in 1964. There were already 24,000 US military 'advisors' in Vietnam in an attempt to stave off communism.[9]

This incident accelerated into a full-fledged, disorganized war that ravaged the lives of young American men who'd been drafted to serve, sent on nebulous missions and provided with no body armor, in chaotic jungle terrain and with little understanding of the conflict's purpose. They returned home with horror stories of hellish anarchy and suicidal missions.

Americans post-World War Two had been quick to support the military ventures of their country. Perhaps based on a feeling of triumphalism after that 'good war', as it was called, the population believed in the leaders' willingness to continue to the point where, nearly 80 years later, estimates of annual expenditures of taxpayer dollars on military and veterans run as high as 62 per cent, according to a citizens' non-profit educational group, figures that don't include weapons manufacturing subsidies.[10] 'Abdu'l-Bahá had warned the world to beware of this very situation:

> Today, all the peoples of the world are indulging in self-interest and exert the utmost effort and endeavor to promote their own material interests. They are worshipping themselves and not the divine reality, nor the world of mankind. They seek diligently their own benefit and not the common weal. This is because they are captives of the world of nature and unaware of the divine teachings, of the bounty of the Kingdom and of the Sun of Truth.[11]

Repercussions of the war in Vietnam affected the consciousness of those at home. Young men, disproportionately poor and black, continued to be summoned, most of them knowing nothing about the possibility of claiming exemptions for medical issues like asthma, or for being enrolled in college as education or science majors, as the more privileged – including two future US presidents – could do. Many at home, among them future Bahá'ís and the mounting number of surviving veterans, joined anti-war protests that spread across cities and college campuses.

Shoghi Effendi points out that America was singled out to help strengthen the Bahá'í Faith in order to challenge its materialistic orientation. He describes the processes at work:

> It is precisely by reason of the patent evils which, notwithstanding its other admittedly great characteristics and achievements, an excessive and binding materialism has unfortunately engendered within it that the Author of their Faith and the Center of His Covenant have singled it out to become the standard-bearer of the New World Order envisaged in their writings. It is by such means as this that Bahá'u'lláh can best demonstrate to a heedless generation His almighty power to raise up from the very midst of a

people, immersed in a sea of materialism, a prey to one of the most virulent and long-standing forms of racial prejudice, and notorious for its political corruption, lawlessness and laxity in moral standards, men and women who, as time goes by, will increasingly exemplify those essential virtues of self-renunciation of moral rectitude, of chastity, of indiscriminating fellowship, of holy discipline, and of spiritual insight that will fit them for the preponderating share they will have in calling into being that World Order and that World Civilization of which their country, no less than the entire human race, stands in desperate need. Theirs will be the duty and privilege, in their capacity first as the establishers of one of the most powerful pillars sustaining the edifice of the Universal House of Justice, and then as the champion-builders of that New World Order of which that House is to be the nucleus and forerunner, to inculcate, demonstrate, and apply those twin and sorely needed principles of Divine justice and order – principles to which the political corruption and the moral license, increasingly staining the society to which they belong, offer so sad and striking a contrast.[12]

Events in the 1960s led one researcher to note, 'The world seemed to be in a period of grave crisis, even on an apocalyptic scale.'[13] During that decade, a social upheaval which led to much social activism had also caused the paradox of the moving away from church while inspiring a spiritual revival. One example of the tumult was the behavior of two Catholic priests and others who were arrested for stealing 378 draft records from the Selective Service office in Catonsville, Maryland, and famously burning them. One of the priests, Daniel Berrigan, later said, 'We were burning draft cards in Catonsville to protest the government's burning of children in Vietnam.'[14] Further, the Episcopal church created a program that channeled funds to extremist black organizations. Between 1968 and 1973 so many priests had resigned that three-fourths of all new ordinations needed to immediately fill those gaps. Tens of thousands of nuns left their convents and parishioners were quitting their churches. Presbyterian minister and Yale University Chaplain William Coffin went on trial for encouraging Americans to evade the draft. Women and gay church members lobbied churches for reform.[15]

Such was the reality of the United States as the consciousnesses of the future Bahá'ís in my study were awakening. I have asked them to describe their thoughts and feelings about the world they encountered growing up – their search for truth, their reactions to the distress of society at large, their peers and their sense of the presence of spirit.

Living in the USA

As a way of capturing a snapshot of the first Bahá'í generation born into the second Bahá'í century, I thought it would be beneficial to record their thoughts in order to observe and share the authentic expressions of some of the early boots-on-the-ground progress of the Bahá'í Faith in the United States. Because I am a second-century Bahá'í who grew up Christian, I've often wondered what second-century Christians might have felt and how their feelings and experiences would compare to the way Bahá'ís today feel.

I structured the analysis contained in this book around a qualitative research study of the lived experiences of a focused population of Bahá'ís. As a doctoral student at Howard University, a historically Black university in Washington DC, I learned the value of the lesser-understood qualitative research approach which came to be appreciated by women and minorities during the mid-20th century because it avoids the mathematical models of quantitative research which tended to normalize white male sentiments.

Qualitative research mines individuals' feelings and experiences as opposed to forming a hypothesis and mathematically measuring the respondents' self-evaluations. The participants needed to have been born during the second Bahá'í century, which began in 1944.

I sought individuals from the United States who weren't born into Bahá'í families, and who were in their teens or early 20s between 1963 – the first year that the first House of Justice was elected – through 1974, the last year of the House's first Nine Year Plan. The narratives I've gathered are from among 69 Bahá'ís who, after an independent search, accepted the Bahá'í Faith as true.

I asked them about their feelings and experiences during those times, focusing mainly on what drew them to the Faith, what prompted them to join and their subsequent participation thereafter. And I assured them that I would not reveal their identities or identifying information. Doing so not only assures their privacy but also avoids making this book about individual personalities rather than about the character of a generation. Having gathered all the data, I looked through it for common themes and then sorted and re-sorted their responses to compare any similar feelings.

The sentiments I've collected through interviewing Bahá'ís about their experiences in finding the Faith reveal various approaches to their seeking which I've categorized into different modes. I do this in order to give some clarity about what might be called spiritual decision-making processes that the respondents had learned, or were learning, to rely on.

What the respondents have shared about their journeys is moving, illuminating and often dramatic. I include their comments throughout this discussion to give a glimpse into their younger selves as seekers and as new Bahá'ís. Although they were in many ways products of the times, their responses show how they thoughtfully and perceptively navigated the world despite its chaos. Shoghi Effendi has written:

> Would it be untrue to maintain that in a world of unsettled faith and disturbed thought, a world of steadily mounting armaments, of unquenchable hatred and rivalries, the progress, however fitful, of the forces working in harmony with the spirit of the age can already be discerned?[16]

After reading through all the accounts, I looked for common themes and have organized the discussion accordingly. These pages will walk you through some of the respondents' thought processes. This statement from one among them resonates throughout the interviews:

> My generation observed the reality in US society during those years, and we became Bahá'ís, not because our parents were Bahá'í, but because we knew that positive change was necessary for a positive life – in the United States and in the world . . . A lot of those things that were going on at that time were very much part of what I was involved in – just about everything that came up at that time.

As Bahá'u'lláh tells us, 'Be anxiously concerned with the needs of the age ye live in, and center your deliberations on its exigencies and requirements.'[17] Most of the respondents were concerned about current events, especially as war was lurking in wait for eligible young men.

Society

The comments in this section illustrate the deep emotions this topic conjures up. The typical rhetoric of glory and righteousness common during the first half of the 20th century is notably absent from the respondents. Bahá'u'lláh states 'every time men are conscripted for the army, a great terror seizeth the people'.[18] This generation was constantly reminded of possible war. In elementary school, even before the Vietnam war, we were listening to weekly air raid sirens, practicing 'duck and cover' drills, that is, hiding under desks or in the hall should a nuclear bomb hit. Kids would come to school with news about their newly installed fall-out shelter whose purpose was to keep you alive after an atomic bomb attack. One respondent recalls her reaction to those realities:

> One of my defining moments was during the Cuban missile

crisis. We would walk to school wondering where to build our bomb shelters. I wondered why we hated the Russians and decided I would someday go talk to them, so I started studying Russian – our school actually offered it in sixth through twelfth grade.

Fear of communism and war seems to have been on everyone's mind. Nowadays barely anyone even knows about the Cuban missile crisis but it was even on the minds of children. And everyone who lived through the assassination of President Kennedy can tell you where they were at the time. My childhood in the early 1960s included the Cuban missile crisis, when my dad was afraid that the Russians were going to bomb us, successfully transplanting that fear into me. In 1961, because he was an army officer in the Reserves, my dad was required to move to Fort Lee, Virginia, from our home in Illinois, as the country anticipated a Soviet attack. There was lots of talk of the evils of communism. Then President Kennedy was killed. I vividly remember the shock and grief of those days. But I was a child. I figured the grown-ups would make everything better and make sure nothing like that would happen again.

Most of the respondents mentioned the mental pressure of the Vietnam war on draft-eligible young men. That young men in the US could be drafted to fight in a nebulous war was a powerful incentive for young people to start thinking and asking questions. For one thing, the voting age was 21 back then, but starting at 18 years old young men were eligible to be drafted to fight in a distant war for vague reasons:

> I couldn't even imagine the horror of anyone that was drafted. There was a very strong sense of dread when becoming draft age. They didn't even know what they were fighting and dying for. Again, there was knowledge of the need for an authority figure to solve these problems and I think we all knew it was going to take divine intervention to solve it. So, many were searching for that. The Viet Nam war was a big part of our life.

Before a lottery system was instituted, where the criterion for being called into service was based on the order in which one's birth date was randomly drawn, all men had to register for the draft and were eligible to be called up. Some thought they'd have more control over their fate if they enlisted rather than wait to be called:

> I could've been drafted but I joined the Coast Guard. When I went down, every third person was going to be drafted into the marines. I had all the paperwork to be a conscientious objector but it was too much work to write an essay so I just didn't do it.

Many young Americans who would soon enter the Bahá'í Faith were as concerned as their peers about the war, the possibility of being drafted and how world peace could ever be established. This sensitive young man had been affected by Bible verses he knew:

> I was deeply concerned about war in general and the Vietnam war in particular and about how peace could be established in the world. I was also personally concerned about the draft. As long as I was registered for college, I would have a 'student deferment' and would be ineligible for being drafted, but the possibility of being drafted and sent to Vietnam was constantly troubling to me.

To illustrate how psychologically complex was the plight of youth, this generation had learned in school that the United States had been considered the hero of World War Two. Some families were enthusiastic about their sons enlisting despite the vague reasons given for the Vietnam war. That is, the US government claimed that the goal was to obstruct the spread of communist governments dominated by the Soviet Union. Public school curricula never included units in history or social studies with perspectives that reflected negatively on the actions of the US government, like slavery, genocide of indigenous people or dropping an atomic bomb on Japan even as World War Two was winding down. Thus the population was trained to see themselves as the good guys, though nothing was really normal.

> That [decade] was interesting. I got married right out of high school in '66. Was going to college, of course. The first year wasn't so much that way, but the feeling that the world was falling apart, in '68 particularly, when I was going to school and working. We had riots on campus. Kent State and Bobby Kennedy, and MLK, riots in the cities in LA and Detroit. It was really that, if we don't pay attention the world is going to fall apart. Not to mention 15 hours of credits one semester. Then I was taking 18 hours of sciences, working 40 hours a week and my wife was nine months pregnant. This was spring of '69. That month our son was born, I got called up for the draft. The stress level was just off the charts. I remember very well talking with my wife about how in '67 you could homestead in Alaska. She was more level-headed.

This respondent had a medical deferment but his three slightly older best friends had all been drafted and been in combat. They'd come home injured physically and psychologically with the knowledge that they'd been pawns in some sort of business venture. The following comment presents a broader perspective about how cultural values underlie the way conflicts are approached. It's an example of idle fancies clashing with seeing with our 'own eyes':[19]

> I graduated from high school in 1965 which was a time of nationalism mixed with generous doses of racial, religious and ethnic prejudice and a fondness for money and violence that made Vietnam and explosive protests all possible when my generation realized we were being used. Americans had always wanted to believe we lived in the most perfect and just country in the history of the planet, and of course that is what we were constantly told, except by a few protestors popularly labeled fools of various kinds.

Every evening on the CBS television network, news anchor Walter Cronkite – who was considered 'America's most trusted journalist'[20] – presented footage of battles in Vietnam. Several respondents hated hearing every day how many of their peers had been killed. One respondent stressed what a huge impression such news made on young people and how it shaped their thinking during that time. Many seekers were inspired to find answers, like this woman who concluded that only divine intervention could solve world conflict:

> I think the Vietnam war was a huge wake-up call to many people seeking peace and there was a driving force to seek a solution. I will never forget the horrific images on the news every night and how dire the situation was. It was so depressing listening to the death count number every night and for what end? There was no good purpose. It made a huge impression on the young people during that time. I remember sitting in high school at break time praying that the senseless killing of our young men would stop.

There were other casualties who weren't included in the official death count:

> I was in college, right out of high school and the atmosphere there was very, very anti-war, lots of propaganda against the war, so the war was at the center of things. At the same time I was a Bahá'í. I wanted to get a non-combative status. They had a lottery. Two of my acquaintances on the floor where I lived got low numbers and they killed themselves. One jumped out the window and the other did himself in with a knife. I had a very high number so it solved that I didn't have to go. But it didn't do anything for the fact that the world was kind of crazy with this Vietnam war.

Young men were the ones most directly threatened by the reality of war and the possibility of being drafted since fighting to defend one's country was seen as a man's duty. Some who would become Bahá'ís wondered how peace in the world could be established diplomatically and were working out their own responses to the draft call:

> We had a lot of kids working second shift who had just gotten back from 'Nam – they showed up in their fatigues. It was interesting, the attitudes they had. None of them were pro-war, all had seen all that they wanted to see. That time was really something else. On campus and almost all of the guys I worked with on second shift were college kids – we were just immersed in that whole feeling of what was going on . . . Me and my two brothers were shooting pigeons and I got on a rope swing and hit something with my left foot – didn't break anything but got bone chips. After a while, the cast got wet so I took it off. When I went to an army physical, they x-rayed my foot a couple of times and I got a 1-Y deferment – I had lost my student deferment. So if Viet Nam invaded the West Coast, they'd have called me up.

My respondents as youth hadn't yet learned the lesson from Bahá'u'lláh that 'ministers of war are insatiable',[21] though they may have figured it out. Instead, the way history was taught to this generation was as a series of battles, wars and changes in rulership, so young people learned that war happens because killing each other is the way it's always been done. A respondent pointed out that this reality caused many sensitive young people to look for ways to bring about peace:

> For as long as I can remember I always felt that killing people in a war, or any other time, was something I could not imagine bringing myself to do. I did not get this from my parents or my church; it was something very personal to me, and I think it was largely derived from the biblical teachings of 'Thou shalt not kill' (Matt. 5:21), 'Love your neighbor as yourself' (Matt. 19:18), and 'Love your enemies' (Matt. 5:44), which I took very seriously. At some point, I don't recall exactly when, I wrote to my draft board

requesting conscientious objector status. I knew, however, that the draft board would not rule on this request unless my draft status was not '1A'.

Not everyone protested the war. This man enlisted, like all the other boys he knew.

> I felt a duty to go into the war. I just felt it was time to do something for the country Anything that had to do with the war was a crisis. I knew people who went at the time, I don't think I knew any at all who came back. Though people did come back.

And many didn't come back. And ironically those who opted not to kill were easy targets:

> I became a Bahá'í after the draft ended. Bahá'ís weren't allowed to avoid the draft but were allowed to be made a medic which means they were dead within the first month. I'm sure Bahá'ís who were medics died at that time.

Of course, the war affected women as well, as they worried about their male relatives and friends. One young woman's response was that during school break time she'd sit and pray 'that the senseless killing of our young men would stop'. Another offered, 'Everything I saw confirmed my feeling that the world was cursed.'

This future Bahá'í was willing to risk his own freedom in order to show his opposition to the Vietnam war but also to war in general. His account of his drastic action illustrates the intensity of thought, emotion and spirit during those days:

> I was looking for a way to work for world peace. I was raised Catholic in a politically conservative, patriotic family. During the late sixties there was great social ferment, everyone was talking about civil rights for black people and women, and ending the Vietnam war. I was in college at

> the time and there were many emphatically-held opinions about the need for change and how to change things, mostly revolving around public marches and civil disobedience in opposition to the war . . . After a year of careful reflection and discussion with everyone I knew, I decided to refuse military induction. I mailed in my draft cards, which was a misdemeanor, and when drafted, refused, which was a felony, and an intentional one. It was not a protest against the Vietnam war, it was a statement and, I believe, the only effective process, towards ending war. I was convicted in federal court and sentenced to three years in prison.

After returning his draft card to Selective Services and being convicted of draft evasion and sentenced to three years in federal prison, his sentence was later commuted to laboring in a hospital. Then he received welcome news:

> And a couple of years later through what I feel was a miraculous circumstance, I obtained a presidential pardon for refusing military induction.

Without the advice of his physician who had experienced war, this asthmatic man would have been drafted:

> My physician, himself a World War Two veteran, instructed me that he was handing me a letter demanding my exemption due to my having asthma. He added that if I did not hand in his letter, he would never talk to me again. Clearly, he knew what war was really about.

The respondents continually revealed how concerned they were as young people about where the world was headed and how they might contribute to solutions. Some came to see the Bahá'í message of world unity to be the only way to end war:

> The 'wedge' that caused my official entry into the Bahá'í Faith . . . was a result of the focus on the need for all of us

to work together in building a new global social order based on love.

In the US, when people feel their voices aren't heard or heeded, public protesting has long been the most popular way to publicize issues and put political pressure on policy-makers. The public at large, seemingly unaware of other viable solutions, lobbied for legislation by any means possible, including demonstrations, protests and strikes. When Bahá'u'lláh protested injustices afflicting citizens, He sent letters cautioning reigning rulers[22] to 'beware that ye transgress not the bounds which the Almighty hath fixed ... Be vigilant, that ye may not do injustice to anyone, be it to the extent of a grain of mustard seed', and to 'Heal the dissensions that divide you, and ye will no longer be in need of any armaments except what the protection of your cities and territories demandeth.'[23]

Protesting also had an effect on protestors themselves who saw in each other an agreement and solidarity that didn't exist in the wider culture, and campus anti-war demonstrations accelerated during the years the war continued. Protestors generally understood 'Abdu'l-Bahá's statement:

> Each nation has clung to its own imitations, and because these are at variance, warfare, bloodshed and destruction of the foundation of humanity have resulted ... man has laid the foundation of prejudice, hatred, and discord with his fellowman by considering nationalities separate in importance and races different in rights and privileges.[24]

This thoughtful Bahá'í put the war in context. He lived in a small town where only a few people were involved in protests while the majority were supportive of the war:

> When the protests of my generation erupted in the 1960s, it started with vocal but small numbers ... the collective consciousness at least of youth was stirred – they started thinking and even protesting injustice, inequality and stupidity.

Seekers probably weren't yet familiar with the above sentiment but all signposts in the United States pointed to this very situation:

> Later in that year, student anti-war protests became increasingly intense, with some destructive violence, and towards the end of that year the governor called out the highway patrol to occupy the [university] campus.

After student anti-war protestors were shot and killed by the National Guard at Kent State University in Ohio, and by police at Jackson State University in Mississippi where students protested the disproportionate drafting of black men, young people awakened to an awareness of a social structure where violence was part of the fabric. This is a good example of the conflict around the country as protesting occurred even at the family dinner table, with arguing on all sides:

> My brother was threatening to go to Canada to escape the draft, my sister was marrying a soldier serving in Viet Nam and I was actively protesting war of any kind. Had I been a boy, I would have been drafted, as my birthday was chosen number four in the draft lottery. We had horrible family dinners filled with anger and conflict between my parents, both veterans from WWII, my sister and her loyalty to her fiancé, my brother the draft dodger, and me, the peace activist.

While there was some disorder and disruption in families and, paradoxically, among young people safely ensconced in university, there was also idealism and active searching after truth. For example, one young anti-war respondent who refused to comply with induction was charged with a felony and risked a penalty of being sentenced to federal prison:

> I was headed to five years in prison for refusing the draft when I first encountered the Faith. I was part of a small

group of Quakers and trouble-makers who refused to sit by and do nothing. We hid and smuggled [draft-eligible] people out of the country, much the same as my mother and father did in Europe a few decades earlier. The majority truly were silent.

This young man had been inspired by the 1969 film *Easy Rider* to ride a motorcycle all over North America. Fortunately for him, he wasn't drafted, became a Bahá'í and was able to fulfill this dream and combine it with social activism:

> Our generation were social activists at a very young age, as far as I'm concerned. That was so important to my life . . . I was working with the Black Panthers' food programs before and after I became Bahá'í . . . [and] spent a year meeting Bahá'ís all over the place . . . we were providing food for Latinos.

At long last, news anchor Walter Cronkite, who had avoided criticizing the US's engagement in war, actually traveled to Vietnam in January 1968 to see the situation for himself so that he could accurately report it. This journalist, who had been cheerleading for the war for several years, now observed the situation and reported from there that 'we are enmeshed in a stalemate'.[25] Although young lives were being needlessly sacrificed, the war would drag on for several more years. The American public lost interest and many turned increasingly to drugs as their morale sank. Finally, the US and Vietnam reached a peace agreement in January 1973. As has often happened in military engagements, many of the US gains were lost and the war had been largely in vain.

Race

'Abdu'l-Bahá gave the following talk in New York City on the day He left the United States:

The obstacle to human happiness is racial or religious prejudice, the competitive struggle for existence and inhumanity toward each other.

Your eyes have been illumined, your ears are attentive, your hearts knowing. You must be free from prejudice and fanaticism, beholding no differences between the races and religions. You must look to God, for He is the real Shepherd, and all humanity are His sheep. He loves them and loves them equally.[26]

Decades later, many youth were disturbed and mobilized by the widespread scourge of racism, whose violence increased even as President Johnson signed the Civil Rights Act into law and schools were becoming desegregated. Television news broadcast regular, often violent, conflicts over the rights of black people to vote and to send their children to the better-funded all- or nearly all-white schools, especially in southern states. During the sixties, the public watched television footage of children being harassed by angry white crowds as they entered their newly integrated public schools; news about the murders of young blacks and whites who went south to help register black voters; footage of white teens harassing black people during restaurant sit-ins to protest establishments that wouldn't serve them and of officials using the powerful spray from fire hoses to deter peaceful demonstrators; pictures of the children burned in a church that was set afire by the terrorist Ku Klux Klan (KKK), murders of the civil rights leaders and activists Martin Luther King, Jr and Malcolm X, the gagging of Bobby Seale when he claimed his innocence of the charges against him during the Chicago 8 (later 7) trial following the Democratic National Convention.

All national news channels and major city newspapers, at least in the northern states, broadcast this information:

> I was a little white girl in a little white town, I didn't watch the news or read the newspaper, so I didn't know what was happening with the civil rights movement at the time. But on the night of April 4, 1968, I was babysitting when

the TV show was interrupted with the news of Dr Martin Luther King, Jr's assassination. Over the next few hours, I watched clip after clip of the marches, the violence, and Dr King's speeches. It was a mega-dose of the reality of what had been going on in my country for generations. I sat there and sobbed, overcome with grief at the horrors of racism that still existed in the USA and shame that I had not been aware. That night was a turning point in my life. I began reading the news, educating myself, trying to find a way to make a difference. That summer, I was feeling hopeful about Robert F. Kennedy's candidacy for president. Here was someone I could admire; he cared about racial justice, he wanted to help the oppressed. Then came the June morning when I woke up to the news of Bobby Kennedy's assassination. I sobbed so hard I thought I would turn myself inside out. Who would be our champion now? Racial prejudice was rampant, and young men I knew were being drafted to fight in a senseless war in Vietnam. We were beginning to hear grave warnings about pollution and long-term damage to the environment. Who was going to make the world better?

'Abdu'l-Bahá pointed out that 'the root cause of prejudice is blind imitation of the past – imitation in religion, in racial attitudes, in national bias, in politics'.[27] In a talk in Montreal in 1912 He explained, 'By this division and separation into groups and branches of mankind, prejudice is engendered which becomes a fruitful source of war and strife.'[28]

During the late 1960s, many future Bahá'ís were concerned about civil rights for black people and equal rights for women. One respondent noted, 'In my area, the social atmosphere was mostly subtle racism . . . I was protesting the racism.' Bahá'ís were notably active in responding to racism. There was a project in 1964 supporting race unity ahead of planned school integration in the fall and some individual Bahá'ís in the South participated in protest marches. By the 1970s, this youth recognized that some social progress had been made: 'I was excited that more blacks were joining, as that showed such promise for the world coming together!'

The nationally-known African American minister of the Ebenezer Baptist church in Atlanta, Georgia, the Reverend Dr Martin Luther King, drew ever larger audiences of both black and white citizens in cities across the country. Young people concerned about social injustices were among those audiences:

> Martin Luther King gave a powerful talk I attended. Protests against interference in Cuba were in the air. What drew me to the Faith, and why I joined: I met an interracial couple whose life in racist Michigan gave me a cold shock of truth. They found the Bahá'í Faith and joined. They told me about it.

After King's assassination, friends in a northern white high school, who'd been involved with a group of students that tutored inner-city black school children, decided to educate the community with what they'd been learning about racism. One of them said, 'Together with our parents and teachers, we organized public talks and protests. We also lobbied the faculty to create a black history course.'

Some young Bahá'ís had the opportunity to learn from a 70-year-old Bahá'í in their community who had lived in their city when it had been officially segregated:

> He recalled days when he would clean trash from the front lawn [of the Bahá'í Center], dumped by unhappy neighbors to show their displeasure with racially integrated gatherings in the white neighborhood.

This sensitive future Bahá'í who wondered what she could do to alleviate the problems of racism and war was labeled by a classmate as a Bahá'í even before she'd actually become one:

> In my area, the social atmosphere was mostly subtle racism. The country was still involved in the Viet Nam war and I

was protesting that in addition to the racism. I was taking a World Religion course and it occurred to me that to solve the world's problems, everyone should have the same religion. Making that statement to about the only person in the enormous cafeteria at the time, got this reaction: 'Are you a Bahá'í?' At first, I rejected it outright. When I realized what the implications were that Bahá'u'lláh was the return of the spirit of Christ, I went ballistic.

There was so much political divisiveness and discrimination towards racial minorities and women that many realized the world needed to find a path to unity. This woman had felt surrounded by people who were more into finding fault than finding solutions:

> The fact that the majority of the world population has yet to discover or be allowed to find the source of this outpouring has resulted in all the troubles we see everywhere and that further distracts people from 'finding' the Bahá'í Faith. [In the] late sixties . . . I was seventeen and looking, knew intuitively there had to be an answer . . . a solution to the problems all around the world that would include, honor and truly respect every culture race and person. The Bahá'í Faith did and does that and more. I found that others at some point subscribe to an ideology that they need to prove that they are 'right' by 'proving' all others are wrong. The Bahá'í Faith does not do that. Furthermore 'others' restrict people from learning about other religions and more, but not the Bahá'ís. I have learned more about other cultures, religions and philosophies since I first started studying the Bahá'í Faith.

Religion

It seems natural to consult religions for answers to the big questions in life. Churches have in many ways been the backbone of United States society in terms of creating stable neighborhoods.

But as Bahá'u'lláh has foretold, we're living in a period of the destruction of old patterns and construction of new ones. As the House of Justice has written,

> Religion, where not simply driven back into fanaticism and unthinking rejection of progress, became progressively reduced to a kind of personal preference, a predilection, a pursuit designed to satisfy spiritual and emotional needs of the individual.[29]

Most respondents grew up in Christian or agnostic families and many of them were somewhat skeptical of religious institutions in general. They say they sensed that something was missing in the messages they received from clergy. By contrast, when they were exposed to Bahá'u'lláh's writings, they were struck by the purity of His words in such passages as, 'Forget all save Me and commune with My spirit. This is of the essence of My command, therefore turn unto it.'[30]

Some of the questioning among young people prompted churches to redesign their services:

> Having come from Catholicism I was not interested in what I called 'organized religion' anymore. But everything [in the Bahá'í teachings] made so much sense, I just had to become part of this wonderful movement, and still am at the age of 74. And to find it all under one roof was a huge selling point, so to speak.

Some said they felt fortunate that by having avoided church most of their lives, they didn't have to unlearn dogma and were pleased to have found a faith that appreciated science and reason:

> I was quite free – by virtue of my family's non-involvement with clergy or dogma – to integrate what I was learning of the Bible with my understanding of evolution and science, seeing the Old Testament stories as metaphorical teachings addressed to people in a time which did not have the kind

of educational tools modern people have. The Faith was the first religion that made any sense, especially progressive revelation. Every single point just explained the true relationship between God and humanity. There wasn't just one revealer of Truth, but a whole progression that unified all religions.

Messages about religion were complex in some families. After this woman's parents divorced, they each remarried. Her mother and step-father adhered to literal Bible interpretations while her father and step-mother were more liberal in their approach to religion:

> I think in some ways I've always been a Bahá'í. I knew my specific Lutheran church – raised Catholic, switched when my mom remarried – was more ritual than Christian-feeling and I became disillusioned. I studied materials from all the large religions, knowing I needed something, but couldn't decide between them because they all seemed to say the same thing! One God, God sends messengers, be nice to your neighbor.

Some said they were looking for something they couldn't find in their church. This girl sought a purity she couldn't find in church but when she was immersed in the natural world, she was able to sense spirit. Her family was concerned about her veering out of their way of life and wanted to reel her back in:

> I had pretty much determined I was going to convert to be a Druid, as I found God in the clouds, the mountains, the movement of flowers in the wind. I thought it was just awe of the grandeur of nature, but I had found my meditation spot. The rest of the family was sure I was nuts ... An uncle brought his Bible over to beat me with it, and was very confused when I brought out my Bible, very thoroughly annotated to counter every point he could make. But since I had been studying other religious traditions, he eventually

resorted to yelling at me that I was going to hell, and me yelling he would be reincarnated as a worm.

I interject the following owing to the sentiment expressed in the comment above which mentions how some people use the Bible as a weapon. Jesus condemns the scribes and the Pharisees (Matt. 23:1–3). Bahá'u'lláh said,

> Leaders of religion, in every age, have hindered their people from attaining the shores of eternal salvation, inasmuch as they held the reins of authority in their mighty grasp. Some for the lust of leadership, others through want of knowledge and understanding, have been the cause of the deprivation of the people.[31]

In the Bible, the Qur'án and the Bahá'í writings, Manifestations of God hold the clergy responsible for leading people astray. As much good as religious texts do, self-appointed religious leaders have been the source of a great deal of harm over the years and throughout the world. Sensitive young people knew that reality was much greater than what the authority figures were telling them:

> I was raised Catholic and was always taught that the Catholic Church was 'the only true religion'. In college, I wrote a term paper on the theme of reincarnation, and for the first time, did some research into the actual teachings of different religions. To my surprise, I found that they all basically said, 'Love God, love your neighbor, be a good person.' So how could only one be true? I was really puzzling over this question. One day, in Art Appreciation class, the teacher was showing slides (yes, remember slides?) of works by various artists. I can still remember one image of squiggly lines and splotches of color. The teacher said, 'This painting is by Mark Tobey. He's a member of the Bahá'í Faith. The painting illustrates the Bahá'í teachings of the oneness of God, the oneness of mankind, and the oneness

of religion.' Click – he moved onto the next slide. But my mind had seized on the words, 'the oneness of religion'. What? All the religions were one? Why, that explained it! I had to know more about this Bahá'í Faith.

A few young seekers mentioned disappointing spiritual guidance they received not just from families and peers, but also Sunday school teachers and even ministers. When they couldn't understand the Bible, they often sought guidance from clergy who disappointed them. A few respondents said they needed to unlearn everything they'd learned, whether in school, church or society. Some pre-Bahá'í youth were often puzzled by their clergy, and a fortunate few had clergy whom they didn't consider hypocrites.

This man as a young boy eight or nine years old had been curious not just about Christianity but also, in the public library a few blocks from his home, found information about Buddhism and Hinduism:

> I read those books, probably understood very little, but I felt that they were saying the same basic things popularly attributed only to Jesus. Nevertheless, not seeing or even hearing anything about Islam, my youthful mind – this is long before the internet and easy availability of information – reasoned that Christianity was the most recent religion and therefore probably most in tune with our era.

As a young girl, this woman had been sent home from Sunday school for asking questions, whereas the Bahá'í Faith encourages and indeed expects an independent investigation of truth. She points out the absurdity of her family that tolerated the dysfunctional behaviors of her brother while considering her the aberrant one in the family. She refers to a tenet in many denominations of Christians being 'saved' by their faith while followers of other religions are hell-bound. Her pure soul bristled at the injustice and the illogic of such reasoning:

Since early childhood I've had a deep longing for true connection with God. I loved Jesus and identified as a Christian, but at seven I was 'excused' from my Presbyterian Sunday school after suggesting that if the Magi who visited the infant Jesus were – as our teacher explained – priests of another religion, then God's truth must have been given to other Faiths. As a teenager I debated with my Swedenborgian pastor about his explanation that people from all other faith traditions except Islam would be introduced to Christ at death and have the chance to accept Him and save themselves from Hell. Muslims were the exception because they already knew about Christ but refused to acknowledge His supremacy. This was my only objection with this dear man. For instance, he insisted on performing interracial marriages even when the exclusively white church committee objected. On Labor Day 1964 I was introduced to Bahá'u'lláh and the Bahá'í teachings, and it felt like COMING HOME.

Some kids liked their Sunday school teachers who exposed them to the wider world. However, this girl became disappointed by her teacher's suggestion that a shallow-minded Jesus would worry about what brand of car to drive:

> When I was around 13–14 years old, our Sunday school teacher posed the question, 'If Jesus returned, what kind of car would He drive and would you recognize Him?' My thought was that the car was a silly idea and I hoped that I would recognize Him. This was at the time of the Vietnam war protests on the college campus. Our Sunday school class took a field trip to campus one day and observed some of the protesters.

Some young people had studied their religion long enough to figure out that some clergy had inserted their own erroneous thinking and wrong information into Christianity: 'The Bahá'í teachings answered some of the illogical ideas that religious leaders had made up and introduced into Christianity.'

Generally, in US culture there is a great deal of collective thought about religion, much of it fanciful, some of it illogical and just plain wrong. Such notions need to be put aside when sincerely looking for answers:

> I think at the time, many people believed that religion was just something you either felt or you didn't and if it didn't jump out and move your spirit for you without you having to deepen and work at living the life, then they weren't into it. Organized religion left a bad taste in people's mouths. I also think people were and still are not used to deeply spiritual content that may be difficult to immediately understand. Most people are used to sitting in a church and listening to someone tell allegorical stories or explain or read oversimplified material on spiritual or religious topics. People wanted answers but not if it required deeper thoughts and meditation or changing their physical desires and habits ... It is not until one sees Bahá'u'lláh as that top authority, does one wish to deepen in it and we have to have a hunger for spiritual truths and a desire to follow through and live our life according to those truths.

Clergy were often regarded with great disappointment because of their lack of insight into real life issues:

> I was dismayed, however, by the political war support of Christian clergy who seemed not to care about the fate of the young men of my generation particularly since my closest friends had come back deeply wounded mentally and physically. Moreover, clergy also seldom supported the noble protests of Black people about their treatment in America, and I had long had close Black friends in my small home town who for the most part were treated well in what was the most liberal section of the state.

The minister and the work he was trying to do wasn't always seen as the problem. Sometimes church-goers were disappointed with their fellow parishioners, which prompted them to quit the church:

> I grew up attending a Protestant church. I loved my church so much that I sang in the choir all the way into high school. Sitting in the choir loft allowed me to hear the sermons which were always based on a Bible verse that the minister would apply to the present-day world. In Sunday school we learned, memorized and discussed Old and New Testament verses and as we got older, we performed ecumenical service projects. I was such an avid member that I even chose to attend Sunday school during the summer. But because the minister preached against the war and was starting to integrate the church, attendance fell and he barely passed a vote of confidence. That prompted me to quit that church and Christianity altogether.

Those years saw a great deal of sifting through many layers of chaotic, contradictory and misleading thinking, and sometimes people became thoroughly confused. After he had served in Vietnam, this man had become a bit nihilistic and cynical:

> When I got out of the navy, I was pretty disgusted with humanity and religion because they always taught about peace and justice and equality. I didn't see it anywhere, including religion.

Culture

Today there's a great deal of derision about the 1960s. It's often stereotyped and depicted in films as a time of shallow, pleasure-seeking people. While such characteristics did exist then, the same can be said about many other decades in US history. Respondents who experienced and thoughtfully navigated those times describe a strange combination of dread and hope with a powerful trend of redefining cultural norms:

The 1960s and '70s was a wonderful time, deeply moving and spiritual, very charged with optimism and hope to change the world. I still have it in my heart though the atmosphere in society is one of cynicism and disillusionment. And the Bahá'í Faith is perhaps more practical in approach now.

Despite – or maybe because of – all the brutality during that period, there was also a burgeoning sensitivity.

> Anyone looking at the condition of the world today will be struck by the dramatic changes taking place. On the one hand is the visible deterioration in so many fundamental processes and institutions . . . On the other is an enlivening upsurge in knowledge, in concern for human rights and in technologies that bring people together. These energies are spiritual in nature and result from the coming of God's most recent representative to humankind, Bahá'u'lláh. He has set in motion processes that are creating a new, divine civilization. In response to this, negative forces have risen to resist the divine purpose.[32]

That decade was a clear example of spiritual energies at play:

> Young people began talking about being sensitive to 'vibes', appreciating virtues like love and decency rather than the more lucrative ones of deceit, greed, hate and egotism that are widely considered practical in a world unable to actually appreciate Jesus or any other Prophet.

It's popular nowadays for critics to brand the 1960s as hedonistic and shallow. Whether or not that's true, the same can't be said about seekers:

> Laws were not something we all wanted. We wanted freedom from that. Freedom from perceived conformity, freedom from laws, freedom from joining things unless it

was a protest against some injustice. It's still like that, but now we're all just so used to it that it seems normal.

The country was polarized between those who strongly defended the status quo, even with all the violence of war and racism it tolerated, and those who strongly wanted to change the country's character to be more tolerant and accepting of diversity. Seekers were of course among those who wanted the country's character to reform:

> My generation observed the reality in the US society during those years, and we became Bahá'ís, not because our parents were Bahá'í, but because we knew that positive change was necessary for a positive life – in the US and in the world. And we arose to work for a better future.

People rebelled against authoritarian thinking and the organizations that embodied it, while also exploring and testing religions for their authenticity and sincerity. Though respondents all come from different backgrounds, religions, families, and geographic areas, similarities exist among the conclusions they reached during their searches:

> To me the atmosphere [of those times] was one of great anticipation to finding answers to all our spiritual questions about life and God. Others had questions too and were interested in those topics, but I think most people had given up on believing there was a legitimate source for answers and there never would be and therefore thought God must be dead, so they gave up on even investigating the Bahá'í Faith.

Of course, these were American teenagers who lived in the age that has been commonly described as an era of 'sex, drugs and rock-and-roll'. Even some future Bahá'ís indulged in activities which they'd soon realize and accept were behaviors that are discouraged in Bahá'í law as not conducive to the spiritual growth of individuals and communities:

My friends and I used to raid our parents' liquor cabinets. One friend had sleepovers when we were in eighth grade and her parents even bought us beer. Later, starting in high school, I smoked pot and tried LSD and mescaline. Also slept with my boyfriend. So, it didn't feel like I was destined to become what I imagined a religious person would be.

Two men said something similar. Fortunately, it wasn't too much of an obstacle for them to give up and replace these habits with a more organized spiritual path: 'Well, I did stop smoking pot [when I became a Bahá'í]. . . after a little while.' And: 'I became a believer and pretty much only had to give up pot.'

Some young people were rather lost, often because of a perceived hopelessness about being drafted and being killed at such a young age. This respondent and his friends smoked pot and took LSD, which interested them more than did politics. But they still had to worry about the draft:

> My friends were all smoking pot, trying to make a living but not trying hard in life to do anything. Some of my friends were a little anti-political, but none of them were political at all. They were just into having fun and taking it easy. I just personally started on a quest – I decided that there was something more than that. Before I became a Bahá'í, I didn't even believe in God for a while, then I realized there was something more than man, I saw the hypocrisy in the religions.

What these seekers were beginning to apprehend was a new awareness of their spiritual nature. 'Abdu'l-Bahá wrote,

> . . . the sign of these triune powers which exist in mankind are spirit, mind and soul. The spirit is the power of life, the mind is the power which apprehendeth the reality of things, and the soul is an intermediary between the Supreme Concourse (or Spiritual World) and the lower concourse (or material world).[33]

It's interesting to see the different ways young potential Bahá'ís approached their search and how they considered their peers. This individual observed that there was a sense of altruism during the '60s that hasn't been apparent in later generations:

> In the late '60 and early '70s, many youth became Bahá'ís, including quite a few in the high school I attended. I owe so much to them because they became my Bahá'í teachers. When I look back on them, they had so much in common; they were all altruistic, open minded and searching for a higher meaning to life. It was not until December of 1971 during my sophomore year at the University . . . I declared my belief in Bahá'u'lláh. Our small university Bahá'í group quickly grew as others joined our ranks. I was not surprised that many of my peers were becoming Bahá'ís. As there was such profound truth in the Bahá'í Faith, why wouldn't they? My only surprise was that there were not more of such individuals. And as I grew older, I sensed that the younger generations lacked this sense of altruism, this hunger for higher truths and a higher meaning to life. When a subsequent generation was labeled the 'Me Generation', I felt that it was very appropriately named.

The period in question saw a sharp shift of values that assisted a search for truth. The 'baby boom' generation was not only the largest one in US history but it was also the first one to grow up with transistor radios and television technology. Direct advertising developed in the '60s and eventually was allowed to target these young people directly, perhaps giving them an exaggerated sense of their importance as well as the sense that what they did could make a difference:

> There was indeed a charged environment at that time including demonstrations against the war, racism, for the liberation of women, and more. There was a rejection of commonly held beliefs about what it meant to be a successful person and an embrace of new forms that included

self-development over material success. Everything was changing and expanding including music, all the arts, ways of living, everything was open for questioning. When I became a Bahá'í I saw it as a way of embracing these changes and the highest expression of what so many folks were looking for. Didn't think it was a conversion because I had already left Christianity and I wasn't anything at the time I declared.

For many, especially in metropolitan areas, where diverse opinions were more likely to be encountered, respondents were more apt to see the kind of response expressed by this woman:

> The strong sense of spirit back then was like going to a party, only some were invited and it could only last so long. Then it became evident that spirituality is finding the power to change materialistic systems. And much of it is within ourselves.

Others, however, experienced something quite different:

> At least in my environment, generally little real awareness of or wish to change, little openness to or curiosity about cultures that were very different from ours – especially in the central, landlocked, part of the US . . . to the extent that social stigma was attached to anyone who was 'different'. Later, moving to a larger community on the west coast made a huge difference and was such a relief!

Television and radio programming made it possible for people to view artistic performances and hear all genres of music. In fact, even today if you compare the silence in an art museum or symphony hall with the chatter in church on a Sunday morning, it seems that the population reveres music and art more than religion. This young man summed up the many trends of the time, linking arts with religion and service:

A lot of us were liking modern poetry, folk music, contemporary art. I was studying Far East Religion. The Baháʼí Faith at that time welcomed newness. The world was one. Peace Corps was popular. Martin Luther King's inclusiveness spoke volumes.

Activists became aware of how television news also conveyed the importance of how images create impressions that become stereotypes of what people are like. Many young people began demonstrating peaceful behavior as a way to inspire positive change, giving the act of protesting a new guise:

The social atmosphere [of that period] was such that many of us felt that positive change was coming . . . I was definitely into 'flower power'. Flower power, to me, meant peaceful co-existence. Give someone a flower to show your love. A kind of precursor to 'mankind is one' in my young mind. Many at that time were also trying to end the Viet Nam war. We believed that there would be what I now call the Lesser Peace in our lifetimes.

The arts often can serve as a surrogate for spiritual awareness: Where people may not be aligned with listening to prayers and sermons, they may respond to lyrics and melodies that touch their hearts. This young man musically shared his intuition that there must have lived more than one Christ-like being:

In high school I wrote a song called 'One Brave Man' about how there was one man in a million who was truly brave, truly kind, and truly loving, and I identified that 'man' with Christ, Buddha, Muhammad and Confucius.

Towards the end of the 1960s a Baháʼí soft rock duo, Seals and Crofts, included references to the Baháʼí Faith in their lyrics. They used Baháʼu'lláh's words as lyrics which they also printed on their album covers, thus introducing a number of their listeners to the teachings of the Baháʼí Faith:

Our era was all about love. [I was a] hippie going to college. Never felt comfortable with traditional religion. I heard Seals and Crofts talk about the Faith when they were on TV. The music of Seals and Crofts attracted me. Their message resonated with me.

In 1969 young people were attracted to a music festival billed as 'three days of peace and music' that would feature some of the most popular rock bands of that time. Between 450,000 and 500,000 people showed up at the farm in upstate New York where it was held – almost ten times more than expected.[34] Although the governor wanted to send in the National Guard to control the crowd, the organizers wisely objected. The event was notable for the young people's peace and cooperation, which contrasted sharply not just with the war, but also with events like the previous year's Democratic National Convention in Chicago, where police brutally assaulted protesters to the war:

> I think the Woodstock Festival was a huge peace demonstration in opposition to that war and war in general. The songs reflected the desire for peace and answers. The youth were so scared and tired of the war and were determined to find solutions to war . . . so, when you don't know where to look, you just start looking everywhere, even if you doubt it's in some of the places you looked. I quickly realized the Jesus freaks, as they were called, didn't have anything new to offer and to me the language of the Bible was so difficult to understand. I wondered if Islam was the return of Christ and maybe we just missed it? like the Jews missed out on recognizing Christ. I found the Bahá'í Faith soon after. I could not deny it had the solution.

The population voiced opposition to what they saw as gross injustices and the government's negligence of its social responsibility. Even clergy were caught in the fray. In my own church, as the minister invited black members to join, the previously all-white congregation quit attending and held a vote over whether or not to retain the minister. Although he narrowly passed the vote, he resigned anyway which prompted me to quit church completely:

> The social atmosphere when I became a Baháʾí was that changes in society were happening [which was apparent in] our music, people protesting against the war in 'Nam, which I did.

Respondents lamented how their churches ignored the war and the racism that were eating the country alive. They expressed dismay over how Christian clergy voiced support for the war and seemed not to care about the fates of the young men being sent to war. Others mentioned their dislike and even distrust of authorities in general:

> I was in high school during this period and was very involved with protesting against the Vietnam war. My other concern was ending racism, as this was also when the civil rights movement was coming to the fore. I had the bad fortune to be in a very small high school in a very small town and often felt isolated and alone being concerned with these issues. But, yeah, everyplace else seemed to be populated with people interested in peace and racial justice.

Many saw a sharp division between their values and those of their elders, something pundits called the 'generation gap' and youth eventually called 'the counter-culture'. The questioning of these young people often led to family conflicts:

> I became more involved in what was known at the time as 'the counter-culture'. I got interested in the natural foods movement and was somewhat involved in the early development of [a] food co-op [which still exists today.] I flirted somewhat with the idea of being atheist, which was sort of odd because I still greatly admired Jesus . . . In that school year I developed friendships with a few people who were looking for better ways for people to interact with each other

based more on kindness than on distrust or hatred. None of us had any real answers, we were just trying to figure things out. One of those people, when she went home for the summer, became a member of the Bahá'í Faith.

Concerned about dwindling membership, churches in the '60s were becoming less formal. Because the way we dress and the clothes we wear convey cultural meanings, and as formal dress was becoming a thing of the past, casual clothing began appearing in venues which used to have stricter rules. Catholic churches were putting aside Latin liturgy and other denominations began introducing guitars and folk singers to attract young people.[35] Guitars became more frequent in the sanctuary and churches endorsed rock operas like *Jesus Christ, Superstar*. But this transition wasn't always smooth, even among Bahá'í communities. Nonetheless, the new young believers enjoyed the camaraderie of their elders:

> As an otherwise socially awkward outcast from my community, it was the welcoming acceptance of the Bahá'ís themselves that made the real difference. The first Bahá'ís I met . . . had been very patient with me. The new Bahá'ís I met were very loving and made me feel that this group of people might actually be a community where I could feel at home. We became a really close-knit family, spending time together almost every day the summer I joined. When I went to college the next fall, I found an equally loving community there. We all supported each other.

One of the respondents had written a memoir about his friendship with an older Bahá'í and shared it with me.

With great emotion Bill Dorrida said, 'The Guardian wrote that one day there would be believers in cities all across America. We thought he meant in the Golden Age, centuries from now. I didn't expect it would happen in my lifetime.' . . . Dozens of high school kids had joined the

Faith at the end of the '60s, and it had made an impact on the community. The small group of quiet professionals leading steady and focused lives were suddenly challenged to open their living rooms and embrace a gang of hyperactive, adventure-hungry, fad-following, ill-kempt, naive, and often lovesick young folks, who had yet to grasp the depth of commitment required to create the spiritual world they did indeed long to see. But their footloose lives meant they were the ones with the free time to make hospital visits. One of the older (over 30!) Bahá'ís shared with me that Bill had been anxious at the thought that the Faith for which he had dedicated his life might now be left in the hands of a happy-go-lucky generation unsuited to continue the work. Then, when faced with lonely days lying in a hospital bed, he found a daily stream of newly-blossoming Bahá'ís appearing at the door to cheer their Uncle Bill. Reassured, he now proudly announced, 'These young kids are great!'[36]

Often when people think they know what religion should look like, it means they're looking for a community that can come to their support. And while this is an important aspect of what people think faith communities should provide for their flocks, such a trait doesn't always line up with the doctrine:

> I know people are still searching, but now as was also back then, people still have preconceived fixed ideas about what religion should look like to them and if it doesn't match their idea, then they're not interested. I don't think things have really changed much in the atmosphere. Freedom and ease is what people wanted. On further reflection, I think the Viet Nam war was a huge wake-up call to many people seeking peace and there was a driving force to seek a solution.

Search for Truth

Knowing the purpose of life and how to live it comes to thinking people at some time. In many religions, even in the most ancient of scriptures, the search for truth is described as a thorny path and a narrow one. 'Abdu'l-Bahá explains in several Tablets and talks how we can come to know anything for certain. He describes the four main ways of knowing – sensory, reason, traditions and inspiration – and finds weakness in all of them.[37] None of the respondents mentioned a feeling of attachment to their family's religious traditions.

There is no state religion in the US, and in this predominantly Christian, mostly Protestant country, religion is not considered a polite topic of conversation, likely because of the variety of approaches to experiences and understanding. Thus, there's no easily familiar vocabulary or protocol around religious experience.

Bahá'u'lláh counsels us to, 'Close one eye and open the other. Close one to the world and all that is therein, and open the other to the hallowed beauty of the Beloved.'[38] It's clear from their accounts that the respondents were looking inward at what they felt was right while rejecting the messages from clergy as well as governmental officials who presented their views of reality and their understanding of how to address issues. Still, there were various types of responses which I've sorted into categories.

God has appointed Messengers to teach humanity everything, in stages over eons. In fact, Bahá'u'lláh wrote,

> . . . were it not for those effulgent Lights that shine above the horizon of His Essence, the people would know not their left hand from their right, how much less could they scale the heights of the inner realities or probe the depths of their subtleties![39]

We're not born a blank slate but have an innermost spirit containing blueprints of our true self. 'The reality of man is his thought, not his material body',[40] and the task of the mind is 'to investigate reality'.[41] 'Abdu'l-Bahá further said,

> This third power is the spirit which is an emanation from the divine bestower; it is the effulgence of the sun of reality,

the radiation of the celestial world, the spirit of faith, the spirit His Holiness the Christ refers to when he says, 'Those that are born of the flesh are flesh, and those that are born of the spirit are spirit.' The spirit is the axis round which the eternal life revolves. It is conducive to everlasting glory and is the cause of the exaltation of humanity.[42]

Spirit is our internal voice that knows right from wrong. 'Abdu'l-Bahá listed the power of the Holy Spirit as a basic principle (the eleventh one in *Paris Talks*[43]) and said, 'By the power of the Holy Spirit, working through his soul, man is able to perceive the Divine reality of things.'[44]

> The world of creation is bound by natural law, finite and mortal . . . An intermediary is needed to bring two extremes into relation with each other . . . and this is none other than the Holy Spirit, which brings the created earth into relation with . . . the Divine Reality . . . The Holy Spirit is the very cause of the life of man; without the Holy Spirit he would have no intellect, he would be unable to acquire his scientific knowledge by which his great influence over the rest of creation is gained. The illumination of the Holy Spirit gives to man the power of thought . . . teaches spiritual virtues to man and enables him to attain Eternal Life . . . therefore we can understand that the Holy Spirit is the Intermediary between the Creator and the created.[45]

How body, mind, soul and spirit interconnect is explained throughout the Bahá'í writings.

The sentiments I've collected through interviewing Bahá'ís about their experiences in finding the Bahá'í Faith reveal various approaches to their seeking which I've categorized into different modes. I do this in order to give some clarity about what might be called spiritual decision-making processes that the respondents had learned, or were learning, to rely on.

Reason

People often hold the mistaken notion that religion in general is magical thinking and far removed from logic, which is considered a tool for the sciences. Yet many of the respondents followed a logical approach during their search and recognized the Bahá'í Faith as highly rational.

Lessons in logic can be found throughout the Bible, Zoroastrianism, the Qur'án, and the Bahá'í and other religious writings. The lessons of logic are so ancient that many think they derive from what they call human nature. Let me illustrate by describing an introductory media class I taught.

I always included a unit on ethical decision-making in news and advertising and prepared exercises from real-world examples, asking students how they'd respond to the situation and include the ethics that support their reasoning. Some would choose a self-serving solution, defending their decision with, 'Everyone lies. It's human nature.' I'd counter such a conclusion, challenging them to present a peer-reviewed study that claims to show that lying, or anything else, is human nature. They couldn't do so because such studies don't exist. However, we can find lessons in scripture that teach us how to reason. What many don't recognize is that the writings and sayings of the Manifestations of God teach us logic based on the reality that our inner nature is spiritual. Human logic too often rests on vain imaginings, which can't possibly lead to sound judgments.

Messengers constantly warn us that our actions have consequences. An 'if–then' statement is logic at its most basic. For example, Jesus taught by using analogies, which is a variation of if–then, such as,

> Again, the kingdom of heaven is like a merchant looking for fine pearls. When he found one of great value, he went away and sold everything he had and bought it (Matt. 13: 45–6).

The message is that spiritual treasures are far more valuable than material acquisitions. Muhammad repeatedly urged people to gather clear, sound and logical evidence so as to use reason in their decision-making:

> When it is said to them: 'Come to what Allah hath revealed; come to the Messenger': They say: 'Enough for us are the ways we found our fathers following.' What! even though their fathers were void of knowledge and guidance? (Qur'án 5:104; Yusuf Ali translation)

Related to this point 'Abdu'l-Bahá said, 'God has created in man the power of reason, whereby man is enabled to investigate reality. God has not intended man to imitate blindly his fathers and ancestors.'[46]

In other words, religion is for the spiritual transformation of self and society, which is hindered when we blindly imitate what others do and think:

> I only knew about the Faith for a month and I knew it was true, so I said I want to become a Bahá'í. He took me to the Local Spiritual Assembly and they asked me questions. I think one was 'do you know what you are getting into?' and I said yes, but was really just winging the answer . . . but nothing was going to keep or delay me from becoming a Bahá'í because I had read enough and knew it was true. I can't explain it *per se*, as the process was not that drawn-out, but it was logical and not emotional and I felt certitude.

Previously, the Bahá'í Faith had been largely unknown in the United States and sounded exotic, so embracing it often seemed like a daring step. As still happens today, many parents worried that their children were entering a cult. Seekers approached the Faith from different pathways, including those from families with no ties to or interest in religion. Many got to the Faith via logic and reason. This young man objected to the magical thinking he'd encountered in church:

After leaving my church, I thought I was an atheist. [I was into] political involvement [and] saw hypocrisy there too. I saw Bahá'í youth for the first time – [they were] joyful & diverse and [I could feel a] strong spirit. Teachings and the evidence convinced me, made me begin to reorder my thinking.

As children and adolescents, some seekers were disturbed that religions would deem outsiders as unworthy of the Creator's help. Many of the respondents resonated with the idea of progressive revelation – that God periodically inspires His messengers with a new message adapted to the time and place of their appearance. This is the covenant presented to Noah in the Hebrew Bible – God's promise not to abandon humanity and humanity's promise in return to follow God's laws.

The Faith was the first religion that made any sense, especially progressive revelation. Every single point just explained the true relationship between God and humanity. There wasn't just one revealer of Truth, but a whole progression that unified all religions.

Despite their lack of experience and because of their purity, young people also reasoned that if God was in charge of the world, then that had to be true everywhere and for all time:

When I was twelve years old going through catechism in my Baptist church. I thought, 'God could not have quit two thousand years ago.' That didn't make sense. My brother had seen Buddhist temples in 'Nam. We all talked about it. We all [three brothers] agreed that everyone all believed in the same God. One brother was enthusiastic about the Faith until he went to his minister.

Respondents talked about how, as children, they were disturbed when their clergy told them that non-Christians would burn in hell and how they wanted a religion that accepted everyone. As children and adolescents, many realized that religions said the same basic things so that when they encountered the Bahá'í concept of progressive revelation, they recognized it. One said she 'felt a loving God won't leave us without guidance for 2000 years'. Progressive revelation is a concept that many people intuit, never having heard the phrase:

> The Faith was the first religion that made any sense, especially progressive revelation. Every single point just explained the true relationship between God and humanity. There wasn't just one revealer of Truth, but a whole progression that unified all religions.

All the respondents remember what led them to accept Bahá'u'lláh's message and enroll as Bahá'ís. And many youth who were seeking at that time shared a similar set of reasons. This young man figured that a man who sacrificed His life and possessions was proof of His sincerity:

> I was attracted by the universal character of the Faith, that there is revealed truth in all religions, that all humanity is in fact one people, that the unity of mankind is and always has been God's purpose for humanity, that God's revelation has come to mankind progressively through a series of Divine Manifestations, that the Revelation of each of these Manifestations has contributed to the spiritual progress of humanity, that our true reality is spiritual, that our purpose in life is to grow spiritually closer to God and to contribute to the spiritual and material well-being of the human race. But as profound as these principles are, it was Bahá'u'lláh's life of sacrifice that attracted me most. To claim a divine revelation is extraordinary; to sacrifice all that one has for it is even more remarkable.

Many of the respondents who were active in various Christian churches found the church membership ignoring current issues. Quite a few of the seekers had grown dissatisfied with their clergy as well and realized that their churches didn't have answers for their questions:

> As a Quaker and of a family that explored ideas, I had come out of a period of despair, disbelieving that there is any possible meaning but had come to an inner affirmation that there was meaning, there was truth to be found. Attracted to the several Bahá'ís on my small college campus by the diversity in the profound comprehensive reach of the ideas that they drew from the Faith, I explored in various ways over time, becoming involved in activities and wrestling with the writings.

Despite the wealth of wisdom in scripture, many seekers had grown impatient with some of the teachings in the churches they attended. Although some of the ideas hadn't bothered them when they were younger, as they grew older and became more aware of the world at large, they began asking more questions: 'The idea of a Big Daddy in the Sky who would reward you for jumping through the right hoops and send you to hell if you didn't, no longer made sense to me.'

A frustration with the difficulty of resolving issues was marked by the contradictory atmosphere in the 1960s of rebellion along with a willingness to submit to greater truths in order to unify humanity.

Postmodern ideas that 'truth is whatever you think it is' didn't satisfy those who really wanted to solve problems. This respondent expresses the atmosphere of relativism that was emerging:

> We were all so conditioned to be free thinkers and therefore believed whatever anyone wanted to believe was good enough and each to his own beliefs and thoughts because, again, there was no set authority in anyone's mind about spiritual truths. It is not until one sees Bahá'u'lláh as that top authority does one wish to deepen in it and we have to have a hunger for spiritual truths and a desire to follow through and live one's life according to those truths.

Some respondents express regret that their families didn't have religion but this one was happy that his family didn't want him to adhere to any dogma. In fact, contrary to what many religions taught, he already intuited that science and religion should agree:

> Also, I was quite free – by virtue of my family's non-involvement with clergy or dogma – to integrate what I was learning of the Bible with my understanding of evolution and science, seeing the Old Testament stories as metaphorical teachings addressed to people in a time which did not have the kind of educational tools modern people have.

'Abdu'l-Bahá says that 'man alone, by his spiritual power, has been able to soar above the world of matter',[47] so that we may become 'free and emancipated from the captivity of the world'.[48] He also wrote that

> All the people have formed a god in the world of thought, and that form of their own imagination they worship; when the fact is that the imagined form is finite and the human mind is infinite.[49]

That is, humans build mental constructs about reality and when many agree on such constructs in a universe of shared meaning, it creates shared mental fortresses that become manifest in all segments of any society and are difficult to assail. Bahá'u'lláh warns us to see with our own eyes and hear with our own ears. Young people are often quite good at asking questions to illuminate any logic that seems obscure to them:

> In that school year I developed friendships with a few people who were looking for better ways for people to interact with each other based more on kindness than on distrust or hatred. None of us had any real answers, we were just trying to figure things out.

Some of the seekers saw religion as a source of division especially because of the widespread impression that there had been war for centuries on end in the Middle East among Judaism, Islam and Christianity.

And even in their own home towns, no matter how small, you could find several churches on the same intersection:

> I had rejected nearly all forms of religion at that point because they had created divisions in the world, been the reasons for many wars and were used to support outrageous social conditions such as slavery. At that point I didn't want to have anything to do with any religion so I may have been the most surprised person of all that I joined a religion.

The Bahá'í Faith recognizes that religious truth plays a crucial role in human development and knowledge, and we must work together with valid scientific proofs.

> If we say religion is opposed to science, we lack knowledge of either true science or true religion, for both are founded upon the premises and conclusions of reason, and both must bear its test.[50]

Of course, young people are often close to nature:

> I'd pretty much decided on my own that I didn't need to be a part of any one religion. I decided that there was a God, that it was all sort of the same, and if I went out to the woods, I could sort of be by myself and talk to nature. That was pretty much how I viewed it. I was pretty satisfied with that. Then I met someone who was a Bahá'í and one thing leads to another. I realized that everything they said was true. I became a believer and pretty much only had to give up pot. Became a Bahá'í in '73 during the first week of the fast, so I started fasting right away.

Others were also led back to religion, finding it to be the best approach to solving the big issue of disunity. But they knew they needed a religion different from the ones with which they were familiar, such as the many churches that had splintered:

> I started becoming involved with the Baptist student group on campus as I found myself moving back towards a more religious way of looking at things. In the middle of that year, I ran into my friend who told me about the Bahá'í Faith. I was surprised to find a religion that emphasized world peace, uniting the world, and eliminating prejudice and hatred. It immediately made sense to me. I began reading the writings of Bahá'u'lláh and quickly became convinced that He was a new messenger from God, and became a Bahá'í.

When discussing religion with people of other faiths, one may be struck by how many have incorporated teachings recently revealed by Bahá'u'lláh, like unity in diversity and equality of women and men. The book *One Common Faith*[51] points out how quickly this occurred. Because Bahá'u'lláh addressed modern conditions, He also addressed their remedies, as reflected in this respondent's comment:

> I have always come back with a clear sense that no other belief system can compare, in depth of understanding, completeness, comprehensiveness, that no other approach gives me anywhere near as good an understanding of myself, the world around me, and the future of humanity.

That many people had thought that Christ would return by the 20th century was really just an aspirational saying. But some seekers realized that the idea of progressive revelation actually meant that He had returned:

> After I became a Bahá'í, I remember thinking about the idea of progressive revelation and the oneness of the prophets, and I thought, 'Wait a second – doesn't that mean that

Bahá'u'lláh is the return of Christ?' Only after that did I find that Bahá'u'lláh had indeed claimed to be Christ returned. I then became fascinated with the biblical prophecies and how Bahá'u'lláh fulfilled them. And then I also studied the fulfillment of Native American and other prophecies as well. I found further confirmations as I studied and experienced the Bahá'í administrative system, with its democratic, non-political elections, and leadership based on consultative bodies rather than centering on the personalities and egos of a few people, in sharp contrast to most other religions and organizations in the world.

This highly logical man studied religion for years, and the shallowness he perceived in reality bothered him, as did the fact that no one seemed motivated to challenge the clergy. When he finally did embrace the Bahá'í Faith, it was because he was attracted to the spirit. Considering the state of the country and the world, the rebellion against prejudice, war and irrational expectations for a peaceful world were highly justified, though many look back and consider 1960s realism as unrealistic:

> I was somewhat rebellious; it was a rebellious age. I did not like authoritarian systems but at the same time believed that there would be world unity and peace on earth. And Christianity wasn't going to be able to bring it about – the concept of new wine in old wineskins. I was told Bahá'u'lláh was the return of Christ and I intuitively believed . . . it was a time of hope. We thought world peace and unity was shortly going to happen, after the Viet Nam war was over. I loved the beauty of the writings; there has never been anything to surpass them. How the Faith has developed! It still inspires awe and amazement.

The concept of progressive revelation can seem so obvious to some people that they find it hard to understand why it isn't obvious to everyone. And from there, they're hungry to know the source of this teaching:

I knew of one Bahá'í on campus – Rick. He wore various buttons on his jacket advertising this fact. One day I saw him talking to my boyfriend, Bill. I walked up to them and asked Rick, 'Can you tell me about the Bahá'í Faith?' The three of us spent the next several hours together, with Rick giving us a general overview of the Faith, its history and teachings. I remember being especially interested in the miracle of the martyrdom of the Báb – perhaps due to my Catholic upbringing. Rick answered question after question and invited us to a Bahá'í fireside that Friday night. Bill and I went. Four Bahá'ís were there: Rick, Nancy, Doug and Mary Kate, who hosted it in her home. They patiently answered our questions, but we wanted to know more. Could we have something to read? Bill was leaving on a backpacking trip, so he wanted a small book; they gave him *Bahá'í Prayers*. I wanted to know everything, so they gave me *Bahá'u'lláh and the New Era*.

Some respondents reported a logical, thoughtful experience, though it was born in some pain and anguish: 'Everything I saw confirmed my feeling that the world was cursed. When I read the writings of Bahá'u'lláh, I found an explanation of how this curse could be lifted.'

Many seekers found the concept of progressive revelation appealing. The Kitáb-i-Íqán clearly explains the symbolism in the Bible and Qur'án and presents it rationally:

> The Book of Certitude was the most divinely inspired book I had ever read. It was clear as day. [After] I had been a Bahá'í for about three months I remember sitting down and saying, 'Oh yes, Christ's return.'

Serious seekers remained true to the purpose of their search. They found evidence in the Bahá'í writings that was so convincing, they couldn't deny it. And as new Bahá'ís they continued to be astonished. William Sears's book *Thief in the Night* has had much appeal for Christians who wondered about Christ's return:

The Faith had answered all my questions, so I felt I had no other choice. Just after I declared, I read *Thief in the Night*, and kept thinking how glad I was that I had done that!

This young woman used both reason and intuition during her search, believing she'd find an explanation about the purpose of life. She began by observing behaviors of the churches and understood how they were interpreting their teachings inconsistently. She was looking for a source that she could understand and accept with no explanation:

> Before becoming Bahá'í, I did not like the division of Christianity I saw around as each sect and denomination was trying to convert people from one group to another. So, my heart and mind were looking for something that has better energy where there is love among all mankind and there is unity among the religions. Plus, I wanted to know the reality of life as I didn't personally agree with their explanation about heaven and hell. I was always asking myself if there is another religion where I will feel comfortable with the teachings in its purest form and not from the interpretation of human beings like me.

This man wasn't interested at all in religion but was open-minded and sensitive enough to recognize the truth when he found it:

> My sister, who had become Bahá'í, gave me something to read and I did. After reading, you either had to say yes, I believe Bahá'u'lláh is who He says He is, or no, He isn't. I felt that the more I read, the more I understood about the Faith, which was very little, but the more I did understand, I decided He is who He says He is and if you didn't think so after reading, there's something wrong with you.

Feelings

Theories about children's cognitive abilities indicate that they mature from concrete to more abstract thinking. Thus by the time children reach adolescence, they become increasingly interested in exploring ideas about God and religious practices. In its letter of 2005 to the Conference of the Continental Boards of Counsellors, the Universal House of Justice wrote:

> Concern for the moral and spiritual education of young people is asserting itself forcefully on the consciousness of humanity, and no attempt at community building can afford to ignore it. What has become especially apparent during the current Five Year Plan is the efficacy of educational programs aimed at the spiritual empowerment of junior youth.[52]

The House of Justice added how impressed it was by the results and encouraged all nations to begin such programs.

Respondents' accounts reported here offer examples of such spiritual impulses in pre-teens. For me, this is one of the sweetest categories because these kids were searching on their own. It makes me wonder about those who maybe never succeed in their quest. Many began studying about religion during their adolescence:

> My interest in religion started in my early teens. I really wasn't interested in Christianity, but I did have a religious awakening related to Krishna. Through that awakening, I came to a greater appreciation for Christ and the Prophet-Founders of other religions. But it was only when I encountered Bahá'u'lláh and realized He was the most recent of these Prophets, the Promised One of all religions, I had a spiritual experience that changed the direction of the rest of my life. I became imbued with the Bahá'í teachings, and the words of Bahá'u'lláh changed the way my mind worked.

In *Paris Talks*, 'Abdu'l-Bahá's discussion about the power of the Holy Spirit is presented as the eleventh principle of the Faith, but people often overlook it when they list the basic Bahá'í principles, whereas it should be a major focus for Bahá'ís. However, a materially-oriented society can eventually machine out of humans our attraction to the Holy Spirit. But 'Abdu'l-Bahá explains how we can access it:

> It is an axiomatic fact that while you meditate you are speaking with your own spirit. In that state of mind you put certain questions to your spirit and the spirit answers: the light breaks forth and the reality is revealed.[53]

It's so inspiring to see how insightful young people can be:

> I was actively trying to understand God, creation, religion. I was about twelve when I read about the persecution of Jews in Europe in WWII, and took that to heart. I was German on my mother's side of the family, and felt deep guilt about how anyone could treat others like the Nazis had treated Jews. That led me to reading the Talmud and comparing it to the Old Testament. By the time I was in high school, I had started going to every church in the city. I was alternately shocked – in the Baptist church they made sounds!!! You would go to Hell immediately in the Catholic church for sneezing – and horrified at what I saw and heard. A favorite saying of my father was 'Spend the week sowing wild oats and then praying for a crop failure on Sunday.'

Although his grandfather had been a Methodist minister, this boy grew up uninterested in church and quit Sunday school as soon as he could. Although he was curious about religion, he paints a grim picture of his assessment of church during his adolescence:

> The churches around me were into names, dates, literal and nationalistic thinking as if Jesus had been a red-blooded but surely a white-skinned American male similar to Superman

who had presented God's only message for all time, and gave the world time to consider it, after which He would return. Even as a teenager, I could see that no one took that logic seriously but, as with everything else, they felt it was a waste of time to state the obvious only to face consequences for having presented intelligent statements about religion or nationalism, racism, and so much more that passed for reality more than 50 years ago . . . isn't that what we see to this day? People know what is being stated is often untrue, but they are too lazy and cowardly even to criticize it.

Some future Bahá'ís were already looking into religion when still in elementary school and did so by reading books from the public library. Some did this on their own, even when not inspired by parents, teachers or friends:

> From a very early age I was investigating Christian denominations and later other world religions.

Some made an effort to learn about religions even during their early school years, intuiting that they'd find answers about life this way:

> From when I was around nine or ten years old I used to walk to my hometown library to check out books attributed to Buddha and Krishna and also Zen thinking because I felt moved to find out if those writings provided any clues, any wisdom, about life. In the 1950s, even in my college hometown, the Qur'án was considered suspect, and no one had heard of the Bahá'í Faith, perhaps because those faiths appeared to be in competition with Christianity and Judaism, which had their own large sections of shallow books about Christianity in that small library. Other religions were given only a small presence.

Children are able to sense the depth of meaning in religious texts and some took their Sunday school training seriously.

Memorizing words of Manifestations is a rich resource as it allows the person who succeeds in doing so the opportunity to think about them:

> When I was in fourth grade Sunday school, we memorized Bible verses. Reading the Beatitudes, it looked like you had to be a certain kind of person in order to attain a certain reward. I decided I wanted to be in the group of the pure in heart so that I could see God. Finding Bahá'u'lláh is probably the closest we can get to seeing God.

Others had had no Sunday school training, grew up in secular families and felt a sort of awakening and an urge to follow their hearts to search for truth:

> I had been drawn to Bahá'u'lláh since my mid-teens. When I was about thirteen or fourteen, I suddenly became deeply interested in and drawn to God; it became a veritable passion. I was raised in a mid-20th-century racist, white-middle-class family. My parents were nominally Christian, but were largely alienated from 'organized religion'. . . So, my sudden passion for God and spirituality came on suddenly, almost out of nowhere. I originally became more or less an unofficial devotee of Krishna and read the Bhagavad-Gita and parts of the Bible; but I also explored other religions, like Zoroastrianism, Buddhism and, of course, Hinduism. By the time of my fifteenth birthday in late 1971, through all of my reading and daily prayer, I became convinced that all of these different religions were, as Rama Krishna taught, different paths to God.

The enormity of the world's problems weighs on young people who feel powerless to fix them. Ironically, as they spontaneously reach out to God for answers, their prayers may be some of the most potent tools in their search. It's interesting that in this account the girl had a sense of ritual that she applied to her plea for world peace:

I lit a candle and prayed the most fervent prayer of my young life, although in words I think all I articulated was 'Please!' I wanted the wars and racial violence to stop, and if there was something out there that would help, please could I find it and be a part of it. In my third week in college, the Bahá'ís listed a fireside in the weekly bulletin, along with their basic beliefs. I think I went intending to join, it sounded so close to what I always believed. And after listening for about ninety minutes, I had the feeling I was being asked by the Universe or God or whoever to make the most important choice of my life. I didn't really know the social laws or even that much about the theology. I just knew it was right.

Here's another youth who asked God for guidance. It led her to the answer of her prayer, one that also resonated with some of her previously formulated ideas:

A few weeks after my fifteenth birthday, one night I was just talking to God and saying something like, 'I wish there was a religion that taught that all of these religions had come from God.' Literally within a few days of that 'prayer', I ran into a Bahá'í who spent two or three hours talking to me about his religion. When he got to the part that the Founders of all the religions were Messengers from God, and that Bahá'u'lláh was the latest of these, it was like there was a 'click' deep in my being, and the room around me got brighter. In retrospect, I believe that experience at that moment was when my spirit was telling me, 'Yes! You've found it!' When I got home, I read an encyclopedia article on the Faith, which gave me a bit of actual textual material to ponder on. Within thirty-six hours, though I had very little actual information to go on, I felt a strong need to decide whether I believed in Bahá'u'lláh, and I followed my heart and said yes.

In an unusual occurrence, an elderly woman offered a difficult Bahá'í text to a young boy. At the time the small town had very few Bahá'ís, which makes this an even more remarkable story:

> When I was ten years old, I mowed an elderly lady's lawn a few doors from my home. One day she asked me what my religious beliefs were. I said I thought all religions were alike. She said that perhaps I had Bahá'í beliefs – she was not a Bahá'í – and handed me a book by 'Abdu'l-Bahá called *Some Answered Questions*. I remember leafing quickly through the book, amazed but overwhelmed by it, and put it back down. It would be years before I would see that book again.

Of course, youth were also trying to get on their feet, finish school and find a job. But they still had time to tend to their spirits. During the decade or so since he'd first seen *Some Answered Questions*, it was as though this man's soul had been prepared for this moment:

> I knocked around trying to make a living and was one day told that I might be interested in hearing about the Bahá'í Faith from a friend of an acquaintance. After having talked privately with him for some months, which included going over *Some Answered Questions*, the book I had scanned years before, I happened by his apartment one evening and discovered that he was hosting a gathering which Bahá'ís have traditionally called a 'fireside'. He was surprised to see me – I don't think he really wanted to expose me to the Bahá'ís yet – and I was surprised to see a very diverse group of hippies playing guitars and singing their own songs, Blacks and Whites in the 18–30 age range, men and women. But the startling part of being there was the powerful, tangible feeling of what I came to know was the Holy Spirit. There was no feeling, no evidence of egotism, pretention or falseness. I felt a part of something very great, something extraordinary.

Inspiration

For years the Bahá'í Faith had been little known in the United States and sounded exotic, so embracing it often seemed like a daring step to people with a background in an older religious tradition. 'Abdu'l-Bahá presents many metaphors to explain the apparent differences among religions. A frequent one is how 'all are recipients of the bounty of the same Sun. At most the difference between them is that of degree, for the effulgence is one effulgence, the one light emanating from the Sun.'[54] He also explains that the differences among religions derive from the 'varying types of minds' of those who receive the revelation.[55]

Further, the Messengers of God have presented humanity with the same basic message but not everyone notices the similarities. Indeed, especially in the United States and Europe, spirituality is increasingly seen as something that exists elsewhere, maybe in the eastern religions. Academic studies into the religious mind also reveal that people are uncomfortable describing their internal states. This all becomes evident in the reports from Bahá'ís below. Perhaps because there's no clergy, Bahá'ís may be more comfortable than others about trying to describe and give meaning to their experiences:

> I had a dream about the Báb one night that woke me up and brought to mind that ultimately it was my own soul and my own decision to make whether to become a Bahá'í or not. I chose to follow my faith and declared as a Bahá'í.

The inspirational experiences of these youth took different forms. What they all have in common is how each recognized their experience as some kind of prompting to move ahead in their current search:

> I was struggling like so many people my age, especially at that period of social unrest, about who I was and what I would do with my life. At one point I had what I would

describe as 'a vision'. I didn't see any visual images or hear any actual words; it was more of a moment of great clarity. I wrote a series of short, free verse poems about this experience. In one of them I proclaimed that there WERE answers to the problems that perplexed the world, and that I was going to find those answers.

When 'Abdu'l-Bahá described the four ways of knowing, He said inspiration is 'the influx of the human heart'.[56] And then He asked how we can determine whether such inspiration is satanic or from God? He answered:

> By the breaths and promptings of the Holy Spirit, which is light and knowledge itself. Through it, the human mind is quickened and fortified into true conclusions and perfect knowledge. This is conclusive argument showing that all available human criteria are erroneous and defective, but the divine standard of knowledge is infallible.[57]

When Ibrahim Kheiralla presented his series of classes introducing the Bahá'í Faith, he withheld revealing the 'Greatest Name', 'Alláh-u-Abhá', until the final class. Several respondents alluded to the power in the names 'Bahá'í' and 'Bahá'u'lláh'. These two young men were so sensitive that they were attracted merely by the word 'Bahá'í':

> In 1970 as a 19-year-old, soon as I heard the word Bahá'í, I was obsessed, couldn't get enough, still can't. So nice to be a Bahá'í all these years.

> Just hearing that name set off a warm glow throughout my heart and I knew in an instant He was the Promised One.

Often, painful experiences prompt us to seek a greater reality. There are several accounts in these pages of young people who had built coping strategies as they explored religious teachings. This young man began searching at eight years old, which may seem young to people in such a materialistic culture but also may be a more common experience than we know:

> I declared an hour after hearing a presentation on the Bahá'í Faith. Personally, I had been investigating religion from the age of eight – my family was unchurched. I went to the church nearest to home by myself, but with a school friend. The church members taught me how to read the Bible and introduced me to the tenets of Christian faith. I had some personal experiences, how to cope with bullies by 'turning the other cheek'. It worked . . . Later in middle school, a class assignment was to write a report on a religion we knew nothing about. I chose Islam. I remember being deeply moved by the story of Muhammad's experience, accepting it, inwardly, as genuine. I remember my surprise that revelation could occur after Christ's time and be valid. I remember wondering why the experience had not continued into modern times. Of course, it had, I just didn't know it. Within a few years, upon discovering the Bahá'í Faith, I recognized the teachings of progressive revelation, instantly. Bahá'í teaching about the equality of the sexes was also a great personal confirmation. However, the greatest confirmation was the idea that the Christian promise of 'Return' had been fulfilled. That got my attention.

Those who have studied other religions were able to compare their differences and similarities. This seeker used a two-pronged approach, studying the mystical writings as well as the practical teachings:

> Throughout my life I have studied the mystical themes of the Bahá'í writings as well as the teachings about science and the pursuit of knowledge, and have always found a vastly greater depth of understanding and wisdom than I could find anywhere else.

Back then, an increasing amount of attention was being paid to Eastern religions. Some Hindus like Maharishi Mahesh Yogi, who taught transcendental meditation techniques, traveled to the US to teach meditation practices that influenced this young Bahá'í:

> Before I became Bahá'í, I was involved in meditation. Maharishi wrote a very simple book that basically describes not really Hinduism but more meditation and studying meditation. This impacted me and made me think. I was working on Hindu spirituality, meditation at that time. I stopped taking drugs after Ram Das said to leave them alone.

Actually, many seekers – including this one – were impressed by both the mystical and logical nature of the Bahá'í teachings. It's fascinating how many of the respondents said they already believed the principles of the Faith:

> I found the Faith . . . it all seemed like something out of the Arabian Nights. This analogy refers to the stories from the *Dawn-Breakers* that I heard as I was investigating the Faith early on. And yet, it all seemed so sensible. Then the 'everything made so much sense' comes from the principles of the faith – these were all concepts that I believed in already.

Bahá'u'lláh teaches that there are two different kinds of thoughts – those rooted in spiritual reality versus the fleeting, mindless chatter – idle fancies, vain imaginings, society says – that comprises the collective consciousness.

> Abandon your idle fancies and vain imaginings, then with the eye of fairness look at the Dayspring of His Revelation and consider the things He hath manifested, the words He hath divinely revealed and the sufferings that have befallen Him at the hands of His enemies.[58]

> Consider then, how all the peoples of the world are bowing the knee to a fancy of their own contriving, how they have created a creator within their own minds, and they call it the Fashioner of all that is – whereas in truth it is but an illusion. Thus are the people worshipping only an error of perception.[59]

We all need to understand and be watchful of the seductive power of collective thought in order to be able to see with our own eyes and hear with our own ears:

> It was the spirit that attracted me and over the years, I have never looked back. I have learned and grown but it was my heart that heard Bahá'u'lláh's call.

This sense of intuitive knowing is the work of spirit. 'Abdu'l-Bahá said:

> Taken in general, women today have a stronger sense of religion than men. The woman's intuition is more correct; she is more receptive and her intelligence is quicker. The day is coming when woman will claim her superiority to man.[60]

Young people were seeking and questioning:

> I was interested in spiritual subjects, not sure of the reason ... my age or the times we lived in? I decided if Moses came again, I should follow Him. The teachings also worked with my prior belief in Christianity.

The way this man came to accept the Faith is multi-faceted:

> I had to investigate the Faith anyway because my family wanted me to investigate my sister who was already a Bahá'í. She came home on leave from the Navy and told me and my family about the Faith, to the horror of the family – except

for my grandmother, who was actually Jewish at birth, though as far as anyone knew, she was Catholic. Because they assigned me to find out about it, I had a big stack of Bahá'í books on the end table by my bed, including a prayer book, and I'd been reading the long obligatory prayer. That night I realized the Faith was true and wanted to become a Bahá'í and told my mother, who took my books and threw them out the window. I picked them up and put them in the trunk of my car and drove away and went to live with my grandmother, who let me stay in the upper level of her home, and I stayed there until I got married.

Intuition

Could it be that the extreme turmoil of the 1960s was spiritually connected with the election of the first Universal House of Justice? As 'Abdu'l-Bahá explains, 'The reality of man is his thought, not his material body.'[61] At the first international convention, when the election for the House of Justice was held, hundreds of Bahá'ís from around the world voted in solemn unity, rejoicing and worshipping. Did the power of this unity affect the collective human consciousness? Some respondents spoke about their spiritual perceptions of those times. These yearnings may have helped them navigate the tumult of those years whereas many of their peers succumbed to self-destructive behavior, particularly involving drug use:

> Like me, when I first heard about it, I assumed it was manmade. It's quite a giant bold step to say Christ had returned. It did not take me long to realize that Bahá'u'lláh was truly from God. But that's just me. About ten people around my age also became Bahá'ís shortly after I did and it was all because of one friend of mine (and also of many others) who was a lovely charismatic young man who had the gift of sincere friendship and enthusiasm which drew them to the Faith also, but sadly, most didn't wish to stay active. I can't say what is in their minds and hearts at this point.

Despite all the awful and tragic events in that decade, many young people were aware of a powerful, almost triumphal, optimism, and believed peace and brotherhood were imminently possible. Some of these messages came across in popular music:

> In the mid to late '60s there was a mixture of hopefulness and deep abiding fear of nuclear war. With the ego of children, we believed we could make the world a better place and right all the ills of those that came before us.

In fact, the palpable feeling that major changes were imminent was fairly widespread. The problem was that such a feeling was mysterious and human consciousness doesn't really support the idea of change, except materially:

> It dawned on me that the election of the House of Justice had released such spiritual power in the world that sensitive souls everywhere were stirred and actively seeking that source. Some found it and others did not recognize it. Yet more found substitutes and some got lost.

There was a great deal of hopefulness that in a few years we would be met with a powerful backlash that some have likened to taking us back to the years following the Civil War:[62]

> Back then I felt like the world, the whole social system, could be changed in just a few years.

We do often notice a connection between our prayers and outcomes:

> Spirit has influence; prayer has spiritual effect. Therefore, we pray, 'O God! Heal this sick one!' Perchance God will answer. Does it matter who prays? God will answer the prayer of every servant if that prayer is urgent.[63]

I recognized [the Bahá'í Faith] as the answer to my prayers instantly. Months before my first fireside I was walking through a park . . . pondering the oneness of spirit I felt from all of the faiths I was independently studying and sent a prayer heavenward that if God could make it so, would He please do it. A few months later, at a fireside . . . I recognized everything was as I had prayed for.

This brief and eloquent account describes the kind of concentration and focus many would love to elicit when reading the writings and praying:

> Reading over especially the more mystical of Bahá'u'lláh's writings refuels me, and it's in reading texts that completely move me to tears that I actually feel that sense of connection other people speak about as love. There are passages like the opening of the Tablet of Maqṣúd where I feel I'm almost sitting on God's shoulder watching the universe unfold, seeing the part of it my little tiny mind can comprehend unfolding according to God's plan.

When he began his search, this young man didn't have a concept of God and didn't really actually believe in God. But after listening to some prayers and writings, his soul was touched.

> I went to quite a few firesides and agreed with the principles, and I read enough of the Bahá'í writings to realize that it was from God. Years earlier I had read from the Bible, Bhagavad-Gita, the Qur'án, and whenever I read any of those, my mind reached a certain plateau: Every one of them took me to the same place. That's when I realized they all were from the same place! I was interested in my own spirituality and the concept of an all-overseeing being, what we might have called the universal code.

'Abdu'l-Bahá has said,

There is still another power which is differentiated from that of the soul and mind. This third power is the spirit which is an emanation from the divine bestower; it is the effulgence of the sun of reality, the radiation of the celestial world, the spirit of faith, the spirit His Holiness the Christ refers to when he says, 'Those that are born of the flesh are flesh, and those that are born of the spirit are spirit.'[64]

Referring to 'Abdu'l-Bahá's teachings, one of the respondents said:

I feel like basically that it gets me in touch, that my mind and my soul are thinking the same thing at the same time. It really is like you just breathe the fresh air after the rain.

'Abdu'l-Bahá said,

Today the light of Truth is shining upon the world in its abundance; the breezes of the heavenly garden are blowing throughout all regions; the call of the Kingdom is heard in all lands, and the breath of the Holy Spirit is felt in all hearts that are faithful.[65]

Here's another account of the effects on a visitor of a fireside gathering:

The feeling in that room was powerfully uplifting like nothing I had experienced before. In fact, I experienced that same extraordinary feeling, which I am not certain was the Holy Spirit, over the next few months which convinced me, even more than the beautiful and very logical writings of the Faith, that Bahá'u'lláh was indeed the Promised return of Jesus.

'Abdu'l-Bahá spoke of the unique character of this Day.

Today the force for Unity is the Holy Spirit of Bahá'u'lláh. He manifested this spirit of Unity. Bahá'u'lláh brings East and West together. Go back, search history, you will not find a precedent for this.[66]

This young man is looking back at the time when he entered the Faith and today, after watching its growth and the way the world has matured. Indeed, people of many religions are more prone today to acknowledge religious unity. As my Rabbi friend says, 'One God, many paths.'

> I did not *convert* from Christianity to the Bahá'í Faith, because I had been studying many other faiths all of my life to that point, and I realized that the Bahá'í Faith was declaring that there had always only been one common Faith. The Bahá'ís themselves were convinced their faith was the only legitimate one, but that was the attitude that every faith declared to every other faith until these recent times when more mature believers share their mutual love of the same God in interfaith gatherings which have been stirred to action by violent actions against religious communities.

Spiritual unity has an attractive force. This young woman felt it in an auditorium full of diverse people in unity:

> Some friends invited me to go with them to a Seals and Crofts concert in our town. I'd seen them as an opening act earlier that year at college, and thought they were OK. But it was free so I went and felt a really strong spirit in that hall, and saw all sorts of people – old-young, black-white – enjoying each other's company. Someone handed me a card listing Bahá'í principles, all of which I already believed. I'd quit my church two years before because I thought the members were hypocritical, so I considered myself an atheist. But at the concert the spirit won me over and I declared on the spot.

Many of the respondents mentioned the strong feeling of spiritual energy that emanated from a roomful of a wide diversity of people. The two college students in the following anecdote married each other the next year:

> [I was invited] to a Bahá'í party for a holiday called Ayyám-i-Há. There I witnessed Bahá'ís of all colors and ages, from toddlers through senior citizens, sharing a meal and having fun together through games and music. I had never seen such a thing in the Catholic church I attended. I decided these Bahá'ís were doing something right, bringing people together in such a loving atmosphere. Surely, they knew how to build a better world. So far, I loved everything about the Bahá'í Faith. But I also loved [my boyfriend]. I wanted to be a Bahá'í, but what if he didn't? I pondered and prayed and waited to hear from him. At last, one night he had access to a telephone and called. His first words after hello were: 'I want to be a Bahá'í!' We enrolled together on the same date a few weeks later.

People first heard mention of the Faith from all sorts of sources. This teen heard a comment in a television program that led her on a hunt as she connected the bits and pieces of information she'd gathered about religion:

> I heard a brief mention of the Bahá'í principles on a TV documentary, from a Hawaiian surfer. They made total sense. I had been searching through Eastern religions, and was ready. I hunted the Faith down then, finding it in a phone book. [I attended] a fireside nearby and read Some Answered Questions that week, which made so much sense out of my Christian experience. Went on a local youth retreat that next weekend . . . took a prayer book into the woods, read the Tablet of Aḥmad and Tablet of Visitation – and felt 'Abdu'l-Bahá's overwhelming sweet presence. I was confirmed at that point. I went to summer schools . . . What spirit!

Fortunately, this seeker had many opportunities to learn something about the Faith on any night. He had been a political activist before embarking on a serious search into the Faith:

> When X was speaking about progressive revelation, there was a beautiful sweetness, and it was as if the fractured pieces of my soul were coming together. The lady asked me afterwards, 'What did you think?' I said, 'What did I think? I disagreed with a lot of it. What did I *feel*? It was beautiful.' This began an intensive period of search. Los Angeles was a great city to be seeking in, there were Bahá'í meetings somewhere in L.A. practically every night.

This person had never engaged with the church his family had joined – in fact, neither had his parents, who were skeptical of clergy. But he had read about religions as a pre-teen and youth and had become interested in Christianity:

> One evening in 1970 I decided to go to the home of my Bahá'í mentor to ask him some questions about the Faith and discovered that he was holding an informal 'fireside' at his apartment. The Holy Spirit was so tangible that people walked off the street to ask what was going on there. There were 20-plus people of all ages and types and colors – hippies, students, working people aged 18–40 – which for me was unusual enough, but the feeling in that room was powerfully uplifting like nothing I had experienced before. In fact I experienced that same extraordinary feeling, which I am not certain was the Holy Spirit, over the next few months which convinced me, even more than the beautiful and very logical writings of the Faith, that Bahá'u'lláh was indeed the Promised return of Jesus . . . Late in 1971 I became a Bahá'í. So, for me it was the Holy Spirit.

Young people often were put off by the idea of a god that looked like an old man with a white beard sitting on a cloud. This one knew that the 'unknowable essence' was greater than the containers that many churches put God into:

> I had left the Lutheran Church at 14 and considered myself an atheist. I had studied Transcendental Meditation at 16, and believed in spirit, but not 'god'. I was attracted to the idea of an unknowable god.

Here's a man who immediately accepted the Faith and jumped right in.

> As soon as I heard about the Faith, there was no resistance. It made all the sense in the world for me. It was THE beacon of light in a dark world. The first time I came across it, it made all the sense in the world. I bought some books, the first I read was *Dawn-Breakers*. There were only a few books you could get, *Bahá'í World Faith, Gleanings, Prayers and Meditations, Kitáb-i-Íqán, Epistle to the Son of the Wolf, The Hidden Words, Proclamation of Bahá'u'lláh*. So, matter of fact . . . I went to X's fireside and didn't get home till two in the morning, talking about the Bahá'í Faith. Actually I had several 8 a.m. classes so I had to get up early to go to class.

Many people had preconceptions about what a religion was supposed to look like and how it was supposed to work. If they wanted to succeed in their searches, these seekers needed to detach themselves from such barriers:

> I think at the time many people believed that religion was just something you either felt or you didn't and if it didn't jump out and move your spirit for you without you having to deepen and work at living the life, then they weren't into it. Most people are used to sitting in a church and listening to someone tell allegorical stories or explain or read oversimplified material on spiritual or religious topics.

Sometimes the rightness of the Faith impressed people who didn't yet know all the details. This woman was struck by a coincidence when she was asking God for a sign and then one appeared:

> I looked up the Bahá'ís. I noticed as soon as I saw them, their 'countenance' had gotten brighter. They all had a light that was growing. One night after a fireside, I asked God what He wanted me to do. I trusted that if the Faith was not right for me, He would lead me elsewhere and my answer came in music. My radio played, 'My Sweet Lord', 'The Art of Dying', 'Give me Peace' all in a row. I joined because it was the right thing to do. My first five years were spent attempting to undo many bad habits and ways of thinking. But I home-front pioneered to establish the first Assembly in a locality near me.

Some active seekers tried out different denominations, hoping to gain insights they didn't find in their family church. This young man, who wanted to find one that was aligned with his desire for an end to war, agonized over what church to join:

> I changed from a ceremony-oriented Roman Catholic into a liberal Catholic, where the Beatitudes and their effect on society replaced the prominence of the beliefs and sacraments of the Church . . . I associated with leading Quakers who held peace training schools. After attending a two-month Quaker program I was empty. I was ardently searching for how to effectively work for peace. I did not conceive it as a spiritual search, though I re-read the New Testament for specific guidance and came up empty. The Bible promised world peace but did not tell how to get there . . . I reached the bottom. I was in kind of derangement. The Bible did not have the answers I sought. What hope was there? By this time, I had heard of the Bahá'í Faith in a hospital where I had worked. A woman . . . told me that the Adamic Cycle had ended, and Christ had returned. It didn't really sink in, but it was the start.

Bahá'ís refer to the Mother Temple – the Bahá'í House of Worship just north of Chicago – as a silent teacher. Here's a wonderful example of a young person's experience in that particular classroom:

> I first heard of the Faith as a tourist, with my parents, to the House of Worship in 1965, and was very attracted during that short visit. I was drawn to the idea that the religions are not in conflict. That is about all that I learned in that short visit, but the feel of the House of Worship had also drawn me. By the end of my junior year of college, I was thinking of Jesus as a great man, like Martin Luther King and Mahatma Gandhi. As I learned about Bahá'u'lláh and progressive revelation, my understanding of Jesus, and reverence for Him. also increased, even surpassing what I had felt as a committed Christian. In December 1967, the middle of my senior year of college, I learned that a friend had become a Bahá'í during his alternative service (rather than military service). My reaction was 'fill me up – I'm ready'. What I said was, 'I've been there. Tell me about it.' By February, I knew I would be a Bahá'í. I signed my card November 15, 1968. Then I started studying the Faith, and was told that mankind was created to carry forward an advancing civilization.[67] As I pondered this over the next couple of weeks, I realized that it rang true and I would become a Bahá'í. I graduated, moved out of state, attended firesides, went to the House of Worship, and at one fireside after we had our coats on, I realized that I couldn't leave without making that commitment of signing my card.[68]

Awakening/Conversion

During second-century Christianity, the term adhesion was used when people stayed with – adhered to – their religion of origin, which, for most (as there were also a few Jews), would have been paganism. At first, Jews who became Christian apparently didn't see themselves as converts, since the two religions weren't officially separated until two years into the second century CE. But those who had become Christians were seen as leaving their old faith and changing – converting – to something else.

Several young second-century Bahá'í seekers noted that they had undergone a dramatic realignment of their thinking which they called a conversion. I include in this category those who expressed strong feelings about the experience they underwent. I personally felt I'd undergone a conversion, not because my beliefs had changed drastically but because my behavior had. I had begun to realign my thinking, and my family and friends noted the change in my behavior.

There's a healthy body of research about the uptick in Christian conversions during the 1960s and 1970s, especially among young people moving into evangelical 'born-again' denominations. One study of Christian experience of conversion found:

> ... all twenty-five participants reported a shift into a new psychological state, with a new sense of identity, new modes of cognition and perception, a new relationship to their surroundings and to other human beings (including increased authenticity and compassion), and new values (including a less materialistic attitude and increased altruism, in some cases leading to a change in career). The study found that people's descriptions of their experiences resembled the characteristics of 'spiritual awakening' as described in spiritual traditions and also by transpersonal psychologists.[69]

Because the word 'conversion' occurs frequently in the research, I asked Bahá'í respondents about it. This woman felt a dramatic change in her thought and behavior when the reality sank in of who Bahá'u'lláh actually is:

> Of course it was 'conversion!' I was Christian and had no quarrel with Christ, grew up in a literate family, and wanted to know more, and began reading the Upanishads, Baghavad Gita. Then Bahá'u'lláh came like a thunderbolt! That was 52 years ago. Bahá is the Unifier.

Youth is a time when people are investigating and critiquing the world they are about to inherit and are often critical of their forebears, who had created a mess for them. Some were somewhat caught by surprise at the changes working inside them. 'Abdu'l-Bahá describes above the way people go along with the state of society they find as well as the beliefs that are handed down. Some got diverted just as they were about to commit their lives to the Church:

> I was a staunch Catholic, considering becoming a priest. I read the Hidden Words and parts of the Kitáb-i-Íqán, and I attended several firesides . . . and immediately felt the spiritual power in Bahá'u'lláh's words. even in translation, and that made me afraid, because I knew this was not something I could casually ignore. Up until that time, I had spent my whole life believing Jesus was the one and only way to God. I spent two years attending Bahá'í gatherings, reading the sacred writings, asking lots of questions, and praying to Jesus to guide me. Finally, I felt compelled to admit that Bahá'u'lláh really was who He claimed to be, so I enrolled.

Several who mentioned having hungrily read Bahá'í writings during their search described their experience with passion:

> I read greedily – John Ferraby,[70] John Esslemont,[71] *The Hidden Words*. It all felt as if the words of the Beatitudes of Jesus from the New Testament, and the walls of my childhood church had come to life. Then I read the *Kitáb-i-Íqán* cover to cover, and all I saw was pure truth. From that moment I knew what and where I was, even though I didn't know where my life would take me.

It's rare to hear a Bahá'í say they converted. It's more typical to say that one 'becomes' a Bahá'í. Respondents describe their new belief in Bahá'u'lláh in several different ways. Notice how this respondent says she 'could hear the voice of God in the prayers'.

Biblical passages about the 'good shepherd' refer to this same idea. 'My sheep hear my voice, and I know them, and they follow me' (John 10:27).

> The first time I even heard of the Faith, it held everything I already believed and I could hear the voice of God in the prayers . . . I went [to a fireside] with some friends and was impressed by the prayers [my friend] read. I took the book to the back bedroom to see more of it and read the Fire Tablet and the Tablet of the Holy Mariner. I heard the voice of God and knew it was the truth. I was in tears when [my friend] came back to see if I was okay. When I told him what I felt he handed me a card and said, 'Here, sign this and you are a Bahá'í.'

There are many ways to describe the process: 'I would not say a conversion, just a growing into the realization and acceptance.'

Generally, the Bahá'ís I interviewed thought they'd come to the Faith already feeling most of the way there. In the present study, Bahá'ís were reluctant to use the term conversion, some saying that it contains a suggestion of force as they associate it with Christian missionaries throughout history. This girl was 14 when she learned about the Bahá'í Faith. She quickly took it to heart and changed her behavior so thoroughly that her mother became attracted to what was going on with her:

> I had my first religious experiences with the Holy Spirit, so I was confirmed about a God . . . I'd call [becoming a Bahá'í] an awakening. But it could be conversion, as I made drastic changes right away, but it was not pushed on me. I had sought it out. It was like being reborn. I put away pot, etc., became chaste, started listening to my parents. My mom even joined the Faith, after seeing my turnaround.

Yet another respondent describes her internal changes when she realized the reality of who Bahá'u'lláh was:

> I'd been searching long and hard. I'd quit my church, experimented with being atheist, became involved with politics, pot and sex. So, when I realized the truth of the Baháʼí Faith I felt a surge of joy and had such a strong desire to follow Baháʼu'lláh's teachings that I drastically changed my behavior. I call it a conversion. My friends and family noticed the change.

After collecting my interviews, I learned of a recently published 2022 study that argues that first-generation (new) Baháʼís don't consider themselves to have undergone conversion because of the theological tenet of progressive revelation in the Baháʼí Faith.[72] Many of my respondents concur with that view:

> I don't think there was any conversion about the process . . . I came to confirmation in the Faith and . . . was transformed in response to it and particularly to Baháʼu'lláh's Revelation. Challenging concepts would work a revolution in my thinking and approach to life. After declaring – in the midst of a teaching meeting and realizing that I identified as a Baháʼí – a process of deeper reconstruction or reconstitution began through a process of tests. The Quakerism I came from was not much God-centered or even Bible-centered, but I remember the great impact my maternal grandmother had in the certainty with which she insisted that I learn and memorize the Lord's prayer.

Respondents were excited to find answers in Baháʼí writings that made sense of Bible verses. Although this person mainly speaks of her logical approach, I include her account in this category because of how she describes the effect on her soul:

> I declared in June of 1968 because of the message of the oneness of mankind and progressive revelation. The writings made sense of Bible verses and prophecies, and it all made my soul soar.

This seeker had been working for peace for some years during the Vietnam war. His goal was to find answers in religious teachings. He mentions how this passage in Gleanings confirmed his belief in Bahá'u'lláh. It says in part:

> Emerge from behind the veil, by the leave of thy Lord, the All-Glorious, the Most Powerful, and seize before the eyes of those who are in the heavens and those who are on the earth, the Chalice of Immortality, in the name of thy Lord, the Inaccessible, the Most High, and quaff thy fill, and be not of them that tarry. I swear by God! The moment thou touchest the Cup with thy lips, the Concourse on high will acclaim thee saying, 'Drink with healthy relish, O man that hast truly believed in God!'[73]

Here's what he told me:

> One night while reading the Gleanings, p. 148 about drinking from the chalice, I realized that Bahá'u'lláh was from God. I made my commitment to Him in that little room in Echo Park fifty-one years ago and have never looked back . . . I wasn't looking for inner peace – I was looking to find a way to work for peace. I found it, and much more. And a couple of years later through what I feel was a miraculous circumstance, I obtained a Presidential Pardon for refusing military induction.

Some people identify with the ritual of church with family practices. Here's a young man who was quite philosophical, seeing his move from Episcopal to Bahá'í partly because he preferred the spirit in the Bahá'í community to that of his former church community:

> I was Episcopal and went to church every Sunday. As a teenager I was not in the religious world . . . When I met the Bahá'ís, that's when I woke up to a different kind of world. We're all hit with things all our life that we may not

be aware of, but sometimes we get awakened and we need to find a certain pathway in life that leads to a place where we'll feel better and prefer to have.

Here's another phrasing by a woman for whom the Bahá'í Faith verified what she'd already thought to be true:

> Bahá'í gave a name to what I already believed.

Sometimes people are so aligned with the teachings, they're able to transition into the Faith with ease. This man eventually served many years on a local assembly and later was appointed as an assistant to the Auxiliary Board. He didn't have the Christian background of many of the other respondents and hadn't been an active seeker until someone invited him to a fireside:

> My involvement since joining has been progressive. I wasn't raised with any religion; I was raised agnostic. I didn't know how to pray, really. I couldn't quiet my mind very well. I learned to pray, to read the writings. I'd read all the words but I didn't really get it. I did immerse myself mostly in 'Abdu'l-Bahá then Bahá'u'lláh, and a few years later Shoghi Effendi. I became more and more involved. I started saying the long obligatory prayer. I went to a conference [where] a speaker said if you want to be a good teacher, you need do these things. And it just stuck.

The idea of progressive revelation enabled Christian seekers to see that they weren't abandoning Christianity and Jesus but deepening their commitment:

> I understood I was changing from Christian to becoming a Bahá'í. I felt that becoming a Bahá'í would bring great changes in my life. I was not abandoning Christianity.

Discovery

Upon reading these accounts, you may have noticed that these young people had been planning something a bit different from embracing a new and as yet relatively unknown religion. The Bahá'í Faith was still obscure enough that not many people, young or old, had ever encountered it:

> I had formerly considered becoming a nun because I wanted a strong spiritual life. But when the priest of my parish told me that only Episcopalians are on the right hand of God, I knew I couldn't live and prosper with that idea. So, I was open to a new spiritual life when X came back to my college after having done a spiritual search during which he became a Bahá'í. We stayed up all night praying and reading from Gleanings. I didn't have a very full idea of who Bahá'u'lláh was, or even that such a thing as a Bahá'í community existed. But a year later, X invited me . . . to a fireside. Seeing youth in action, feeling the presence of love for God, discovering that Bahá'u'lláh wasn't 'replacing' Christ but fulfilling Christianity, [reading] Portals to Freedom, and [hearing] a Seals and Crofts concert in a Catholic girls' school gym all guided me to want to be a Bahá'í.

Sometimes it took a while before people completely settled into the life-changing choice they had made. During the 1960s, smoking pot had spread deep into the middle class and had become more common than it was during our parents' generation:

> When I declared I had to make a deal with God. I wanted to be sure, and I didn't feel sure after all the firesides, reading, talking and praying. I just couldn't go to Feast. So, I told God I would declare for a year and see if that brought me the certainty I was looking for. A couple of months later, while talking to a seeker, I stopped in mid-sentence and said, 'Wow, I really believe this stuff!' I had found the certitude somewhere along the way.

The following path is tough to categorize but seems mostly intuitive. This girl had done enough research to know something about the faith of the ancient Druids. In the natural world, one is surrounded by the purity of living beings. Perhaps the Japanese term 'forest bathing'[74] – taking in the forest atmosphere – describes her feeling. Her account, though somewhat tongue-in-cheek, describes the kind of turmoil that was visiting many US households. She indicates the sort of courage new Bahá'í youth had when they told their parents they'd joined a new religion. Her humorous tone seems to reflect some joy and bewilderment about what she'd found. You'll also notice the resolve of her friend who insisted that she go to a fireside with him:

> [Our family] had all the joys of the late '60s – alcoholism, a hippie with drug problems, sexual abuse, poverty. And I was the problem because I didn't smoke, drink, play around, use drugs, swear. I was the black sheep, and an intervention was planned to bring me back into the fold . . . In my senior year, 1970, I met a young man who had transferred from Germany. He was handsome, smart, kind, and I was deeply in lust for him. We had a few classes together and had talked a lot about things we thought were important, and he invited me to a Bahá'í fireside. I said no, not interested. He said he would pick me up. I said not necessary, I was a Druid. He was at my house at seven p.m. Friday, and I went with him. At the end of the fireside, I knew four things absolutely. The Faith was started by a man named Bob, there was a secret password to enter (Alláh-u-Abhá), and there was a guy who was writing letters and wanted to be my brother (Shoghi Effendi). And that I was a Bahá'í. I was wrong about the first three and had no idea the implications of the truth of the fourth.

Fulfillment

Many respondents perceived their moving from Christianity into the Bahá'í Faith as an extension of what they'd already believed. They rationally and prayerfully recognized their embrace of the Faith as fulfillment, not a conversion, which for them had a connotation of being forced. 'Becoming a Bahá'í was not a conversion for me. Rather, it was confirmation of what I knew had to be true.' This young man was immersed in constant social changes, like the war, racism, America's history of hypocrisy. He eventually saw religion as a way to explain the turmoil and create stability. Having studied the Bible and knowing about its prophecies, several felt that the coming of Bahá'u'lláh had solved that puzzle. 'I felt that Bahá'í was the fulfillment of biblical prophecies, so I was not converted, I was not giving up anything.'

It was logical to many that a loving God would not leave anyone in the world in darkness. And it made sense to them that someone as great as Christ could solve the mess in the world. These three individuals all rejected the idea that they had converted. It seems that they balanced what they intuited must be true against the reality of the Faith. Here are several more responses about conversion:

> I was twenty-five when I heard about this Faith and studied to disprove it but joined and I called it a graduation because my view had changed to a Bahá'í view. Conversion? No, just graduated.

> Keeping up, rather than a conversion.

> Everything I learned about the Faith went along with what I had always believed, so no, not a conversion, more an extension or an addition.

> Bahá'í gave a name to what I already believed.

Here's someone who appreciated his Quaker affiliation but was detached enough from it to be able to recognize Bahá'u'lláh as presenting the truth:

I decided I had to investigate Bahá'u'lláh and figure out if He indeed was the Messenger He claimed to be. After months of study and fervent prayer, I decided that He was. I still wanted to be a Quaker, but I had to be a Bahá'í. I do not think of it as a 'conversion'. I think of it as recognizing the Messenger of God for this Day.

Some souls are well prepared by the time they encounter Bahá'í teachings:

> [An acquaintance] invited me to a fireside. The speaker introduced progressive revelation. Three weeks later I signed my card.

Another had sought a strong spiritual life amid his religious community, acknowledges that it was necessary to be dedicated and sincere, and alludes to the difficulty of the search. 'It was the religion I had been looking for. So glad I found it.'

Considering the idiosyncrasies of individuals' spiritual paths should give a sense of their diverse approach to problem-solving in general:

> The principles are practical, logical and actionable. Bahá'u'lláh is the source and I knew it was true. I had been thinking about it for some time. But as close as I can come to a feeling with Asperger's is to say all my logic and rational thinking gave me certitude that this was ALL true, and later I learned more about being excited and motivated from within to take more action. I guess all I did was know that it was true rather than a wave of emotion, tears, shaking, fainting or feeling something.

This woman summarizes how her search has carried forward into her life as a Bahá'í, in a constant feeling of search:

> After three months of reading and going to firesides, I accepted that the principles made sense and resonated with

me. I would not say a conversion, just a growing into the realization and acceptance. Since then, over the last fifty-two years I have continued to grow spiritually and fallen more deeply in love and more committed. And the commitment becomes stronger as the years pass with devotion to service. And always I have felt 'it doesn't get any better than this' and it does!

4
Second Century Believers

Shoghi Effendi wrote,

> Though small in numbers and circumscribed as yet in your experience, powers, and resources, yet the Force which energizes your mission is limitless in its range and incalculable in its potency.[1]

In describing the Bahá'í Faith, Shoghi Effendi's language often expands on the meaning of religion, which is usually seen as a body of scripture and ritual. Shoghi Effendi frequently referred to the Bahá'í Faith as a Cause, as does the Universal House of Justice. Whereas the word 'religion' is loaded with historical baggage, the word 'Cause' better describes a Bahá'í understanding of what 'religion' is – the dedicated effort of like-minded people. It encompasses the universal breadth and depth of what God's Messengers have always intended for humankind.

Even more challenging than finding the Faith is living it. This involves coming together in community with fellow believers, studying the teachings of Bahá'u'lláh and the Báb, and the guidance of 'Abdu'l-Bahá, Shoghi Effendi and the Universal House of Justice, helping to form and develop the young institutions and sharing the teachings with others.

New Bahá'ís found themselves immersed in a new kind of community. Once people enter into the Bahá'í Faith they become part of an order that is based on individuals freely consulting, volunteering to serve, and taking charge of their own spiritual growth. While it's true that fellow members have varying levels of knowledge, wisdom, talent, experience and ability, no one person is of a higher status or in a position to give the final word on the meaning of the scripture. Such status belongs only to the writings and the interpretations of 'Abdu'l-Bahá and Shoghi Effendi, and all of our understandings vary.

Many seekers had been attracted by the loving and unified community they found where they could feel a powerful spirit. Just the mere gathering of Bahá'ís was a new experience for many of the respondents because of the communities' wide diversity of ages, races, interests, education levels and religious backgrounds. Over the years they've come to realize that such a feeling in their communities is the result of community members making a sincere effort to show their mutual appreciation of and concern for each other:

> The first thing I learned was the Faith is not the Bahá'ís and that all Bahá'ís are learning like everyone else. An incident that made me uncomfortable should not be a reason to no longer go to Feasts. That lesson stuck with me and I often remind new Bahá'ís to keep their eyes and heart focused on the Central Figures – not on Bahá'ís. I remind them everyone is in a different place on the path and we can only be concerned with our own growth. There have been many changes in the Faith as we have grown together. What keeps me is the first-hand experience, that God has a plan that we will never fully grasp, but He has shared it with us. The plan to help mankind grow to the next level of development by following Bahá'u'lláh's instructions has to be shared far and wide.

Working in groups is built into the fabric of the Bahá'í Faith; members of institutions are urged to consult until they reach consensus and, if they cannot reach consensus, they are to vote. Following the tenets of Bahá'í consultation renders it unlike any models in the secular world:

> One of the things about why I joined, I realized that if we're going to make the world a better place, it was better working together than people trying to do it on your own.

Community also includes the basic building block of family. For some Bahá'ís, parents were less than supportive about their own offspring choosing an unfamiliar path. Youth who grew up in a family that wasn't Bahá'í sometimes faced a dilemma when and if their family opposed their participation: 'My family went nuts; it was horrible.'

Actually, the youth may have been less than gentle as they tried to live their new faith in their same old households. This was something they needed to negotiate. For instance, some were uncertain how to observe Christmas or Easter. And sometimes the parents were so shaken by learning their child had joined a relatively unknown religion, they jumped to wrong assumptions:

> Oddly, in my own family, my father assumed until the day he died that I had become a Muslim. And in his later years he used to warn me about how the Taliban treat 'their women'.

Experiencing a true unity in diversity can be startling as it produces a strong sense of unity, especially when you witness close feelings among types of people whom you never imagined would socialize with each other:

> Where I was . . . there was a definite 'flower children' atmosphere about the community, which attracted me. I was first attracted by the love and unity and the immediate acceptance and warm inclusion.

Still, Bahá'ís learn that they can't judge the Revelation by the behavior of other Bahá'ís who may sometimes disappoint them. Respondents mentioned the difficulties of learning to do this work with so many diverse types. Because there's no clergy, Bahá'ís often can't avoid each other and must learn to work out their differences in a consultative way as well as learn new behaviors and attitudes for which they may consult the writings. They also may turn to Board members and Local Assemblies for help dealing with personal and interpersonal problems. The Bahá'í writings provide guidance and inspiration for such situations and one can always write to the elected world body for clarification, guidance and assistance.

In practice, however, Bahá'ís generally learn how to use consultation to work out difficulties and differences of opinion. Our only real differences are in our thoughts, not in our appearances or behaviors. In diverse communities, people learn to be watchful of how they say things:

> It wasn't until I had been a Bahá'í for some years that I became troubled by the terms 'American Bahá'í' or 'Iranian Bahá'í' or 'Japanese Bahá'í'. My understanding had always been that we were trying to establish a new world order without these divisions or differences. I was trying to raise my children to be part or a new culture – the Bahá'í culture. It still disturbs me to hear these terms.

New Bahá'ís are often warned that fellow Bahá'ís are not the Faith itself. The writings remind us that we need to develop spiritual attributes, which our differences with others constantly test.

> I have been very tested by individual Bahá'ís and by Bahá'í communities and have sometimes suffered disappointment – such as my Bahá'í teacher leaving the Faith, or not feeling accepted in terms of my [contributions] – but I never lost belief in the Central Figures of the Faith.

Of course, Bahá'ís are human like everyone else and have to deal with each other in the community, which is challenging with so much diversity:

> I was shocked at her anger and she did not explain and I got real quiet and just walked away and sat in the bleachers for a while trying to figure it out. I didn't and was still confused as I walked back to the dorm . . . Bahá'u'lláh protected me

when I needed help. My faith in Bahá'u'lláh is strengthened every time this happens.

Looking back at himself as a young man trying to obey instructions, this individual thinks he should have perhaps used more wisdom but hadn't had the perspective or knowledge to have known better choices:

> Perhaps a dozen or so youth like myself shared the Faith in [our state] which, even in the 1970s, was at least mentally segregated. Many people, Black and White, became Bahá'ís at that time, and at least one Black man said he would love to become a Bahá'í, but the local people would make his life very difficult if he did so. Looking back, I realize that our approach, full of youthful enthusiasm and insensitivity, overlooked the wiser approach of 'Abdu'l-Bahá. Signing a declaration card never meant anything; becoming sensitive to the Holy Spirit meant everything.

Having experienced periods of growth as well as periods of drought, this man has made some observations about human behavior and how rocky is the path:

> The young man that taught me initially about the Faith would eventually caution that the members of the Bahá'í community were not perfect. Well, neither he nor I were perfect either, and I was never concerned about anyone else's condition, because you see that everywhere in your life anyway. Not so for many community members who withdrew over time, because someone they had revered failed to fulfill their exalted reputation. Moreover, I learned that no religious community has ever, will ever, be that Faith any more than the patients in a hospital are its exemplars. Fortunately, I have been privileged to know wonderful examples of indigenous American, Hindu, Zoroastrian, Jewish, Buddhist, Christian, Sikh, Muslim and Bahá'í Faiths, all of whom are aware of the tangible Holy Spirit

which is denied existence by intellectual dullards afraid of Reality.

Sometimes guidance may not have been received as intended. During the 1960s–1970s as an influx of people entered the Baháʼí Faith, goals were set to organize them into Local Spiritual Assemblies (LSAs), the foundation of the administrative framework. When a legal jurisdiction reaches nine Baháʼí members, these members can form and legally incorporate a LSA. There were instances where new young Baháʼí teachers might find nine individuals in a jurisdiction who considered themselves Baháʼís which led the teachers to wrongly think they could consider them an LSA. This is an example of a practice that would have been better avoided:

> I'm usually the quiet third wheel and I helped form 'paper Assemblies' by going out and finding the new Baháʼís and explaining to them that we needed their signature and eight others to form an Assembly. I think we did this for a week. They never got all nine community members together to elect officers, thus 'paper Assemblies'. That is how we met the goal.

Perhaps growth means something besides the number of Baháʼís, or the number of assemblies. That is, maybe it means the magnitude of individual spiritual growth. One individual cited this letter of Shoghi Effendi to the Antipodes:

> Shoghi Effendi wishes me to acknowledge the receipt of your letter dated February 20th 1932 . . . We wish we had people, truly Baháʼí in spirit, who would travel from one city to another, meet the friends, cheer their hearts & stimulate them to further activity. They would be rendering such a service, even though they make no speeches & actually teach no one, for the keeping up of the hopefulness & spirit of the friends is an important enough job.[2]

It's often difficult to find the time or inclination to meet with each other just to be together and share love and encouragement, especially if we don't enjoy some people's personalities or truly appreciate their differences:

> My behavior has always been the problem because [people with Asperger's] will not act 'normal' unless they are acting. We are wired differently and it does not change. It is neurodivergent and normal. But it conflicts with a lot of the Bahá'ís' expectations and social norms. Where unity is 'everyone doing the same thing the same way at the same time', there was little room for individual initiative . . . Actually, the Asperger's was a saving grace because I did not care about the emotional support or not.

The Bahá'í Faith is a covenantal religion. What this means is that when someone asks to become a member of this religion, they're agreeing that they recognize that Bahá'u'lláh is who He says He is and that as a member of the Faith they will obey His laws and ordinances.

A prayer of 'Abdu'l-Bahá says,

> O my Lord and my Hope! Help Thou Thy loved ones to be steadfast in Thy mighty Covenant, to remain faithful to Thy manifest Cause, and to carry out the commandments Thou didst set down for them in Thy Book of Splendors; that they may become banners of guidance and lamps of the Company above, wellsprings of Thine infinite wisdom, and stars that lead aright, as they shine down from the supernal sky.[3]

Individual Bahá'ís may be elected or appointed to serve on an institution, so because the Bahá'í Faith lacks clergy and requires its members to participate at all levels of the Administration, avowed believers sooner or later realize that they need to focus on the guidance.

There is a range of people who eventually fade away – all

because they see the Bahá'í Faith as merely a social movement, rather than what it really is – the latest revelation from God. Arguably, the heart of the problem with such people is that they don't understand who and what a Manifestation of God is; they see Him as a philosopher, a reformer, a guy who was ahead of his time, et cetera. They don't see Him as one who is the embodiment of all of the infinite number of divine attributes which come from the divine and unknowable Essence, and which find their highest expression solely in the person of the Manifestation.

Relationships with First Century Bahá'ís

Biographies have been written about many of the better-known first-century Bahá'ís, such as those who met 'Abdu'l-Bahá and those moving to other countries where there were no Bahá'ís and struggled to build local assemblies and communities. It's worth pointing out that there were also those who remained in the US and were caught off-guard by the sudden influx of youth during the 1960s and 1970s who weren't from Bahá'í families. In this passage, *Century of Light* mentions this generation of youth and their elders:

> The 1960s and 1970s were heady days for a Bahá'í community most of whose growth outside of Iran had been slow and measured . . . Following in the path that these extraordinary figures had opened, thousands of young Bahá'ís arose in subsequent years to proclaim the message of the Faith throughout all five continents and the scattered islands of the globe . . . The spirit of zeal and enthusiasm characteristic of youth has also provided an ongoing challenge to the general body of the community to explore ever more audaciously the revolutionary social implications of Bahá'u'lláh's teachings.[4]

Young people attracted to the Faith necessarily encountered and formed relationships with the older generation – and vice versa:

The very first Bahá'í function I went to was an Ayyam-i-Há party at [the local] college. It impressed me that there were people my age and older people and everyone interacted comfortably with one another. That was impressive to me because it wasn't anything you saw elsewhere. I didn't pay much attention to the Faith but was impressed that they were talking with one another.

In the culture back then, it was unusual for teens to form friendships with unrelated adults who weren't family friends or teachers. Although the Bahá'í Faith has no official status equivalent to church 'elder', Bahá'í youth intuited that they could learn much from the experiences of older Bahá'ís and fondly recall those relationships. This unusual interaction gave pause to this young man who never forgot the incident:

> I went street teaching with Marguerite Hipsley who'd sat on 'Abdu'l-Bahá's lap as a child. I appreciate it because [those elders] were around and stayed with it for all those years. I remember Albert James, an Auxiliary Board Member who visited our community and he said he could tell when people say their long obligatory prayer . . . I remember a Knight of Bahá'u'lláh who said he was in London and thought, 'Look at all these people walking around who don't know Bahá'u'lláh.' Then he looked and saw a glow from a guy and realized he'd been to a fireside. I felt like there was hope and that the future looked promising.

As this woman says, the first-century Bahá'ís enchanted the youth with their stories of the early days of the Faith:

> A member of our community had met 'Abdu'l-Bahá when she was a young adult. She didn't talk about it often; it was a brief meeting. It made me feel how young the Faith is, and how we are involved in the beginning of it – especially the beginning of the administrative order. For some time I

didn't realize Shoghi Effendi wasn't still living – a result of his influence on the older Bahá'ís.

Youth heard a treasure trove of stories from the diverse people they were encountering in their Bahá'í communities. They were meeting so many different kinds of people they never would have met had they stayed in their family churches:

> I moved to a border city, meaning that it had been a segregated city and Jim Crow laws excluded blacks from public facilities that whites used – schools, jobs, stores, restaurants and neighborhoods were segregated. I met Albert James who became a Bahá'í in 1934. He told me his story. He was the only black Bahá'í there until World War II. A Bahá'í who lived in all-white Highlandtown helped James find a job. But it was difficult for the white Bahá'ís to make contact with the black community. They'd been able to sponsor an illustrated lecture on the Bahá'í Temple, entitled 'The Temple of Light', at a local historically black college and also at the main public library. A few made efforts to teach in the black neighborhoods, but not until World War II did strict barriers of race and class begin to weaken.

Here is another example of how members of this rebellious generation were transformed by friendships with longtime Bahá'ís. This respondent offered to share his memoir in which he had expressed the kinds of feelings and experiences I'd asked about. Had he allowed his prejudices to keep him away from chatting with an older man, his life might have taken a different turn. Instead, this is where he first learned about the Faith.

> I agreed to accompany my girlfriend to the . . . State Fair where she had volunteered to stroll the crowd and hand out political literature . . . I saw a smaller booth with one attendant, an older gentleman. Dutifully, I offered him one of the pamphlets we carried. His response surprised me. 'I'll take one of yours if you'll take one of mine.' How could

I have suspected, with those words, the course of my life had just been altered? . . . [He] gave me a pamphlet with the basic principles of the Baháʼí Faith and my interest was immediately sparked. I asked questions and his patient explanations were so 'far out' as we would say in those days . . . that I felt like I'd stumbled upon a secret fountain of truth. I could feel new vistas opening before me . . . I had a vague notion that ending the Vietnam war would somehow right the troubled world. But [he] was talking of much broader solutions – the equality of men and women, a universal auxiliary language, the elimination of the extremes of wealth and poverty, the harmony of science and religion. 'The earth is but one country, and mankind its citizens.' Could I really be hearing this from an old guy wearing a tie? My generation's mantra was, 'Don't trust anyone over 30!'[5]

Not only did this woman hear first-hand accounts of black people's experiences during legal segregation, she also learned more details about what their daily lives were like:

I was moved by the determination of an older black Baháʼí who explained to me the difficulties of traveling and how black people had to use the *Green Book*[6] while traveling in order to locate hotels and motels where they'd be able to get rooms. When he and his family traveled to Chicago, they found their hotel reservations weren't honored when the hotel manager saw they were black. He recalled how his Chicago friend suggested they try Evanston, where they did get a room. His friend also suggested they go up to visit the newly completed Baháʼí House of Worship in nearby Wilmette. Then back home, they continued to investigate the Faith by attending regular Friday night firesides at a home in an all-white neighborhood where blacks might be arrested if found on the streets after dark. One of the white people accompanied them and both were at risk of being arrested. After a year and a half, he and his wife declared.

So many of the youth who entered the Faith were accustomed to disagreeing with their elders and questioning the status quo on every issue. They were growing up in a world with different expectations and experiences than the previous generations and with a different aesthetic. Youth learned that in some communities their clothing style presented a problem for the older generation and they were counseled not to wear blue jeans to Feast. Still, the significant influx of youth entering the Faith were welcomed, incorporated and nurtured by first-century Bahá'ís who shared stories of the old days, such as about the messages from the Guardian to the National Assembly who shared them with communities to read at Feast. Some young Bahá'ís were privileged to meet elders with vast experience in the Faith:

> Those long-term Bahá'ís really shaped my life. I met some who served on Assemblies when the Guardian died and Mason Remey made his announcement. What a difficult time that was! I met several who had pioneered and were very deepened in the writings. I really miss those folks and it is now up to us to convey that faith to the new young believers. I fear we may not be doing a good job at that. Look at how few new believers there are. Back then there were thousands. Now there is barely one declaration per month per state.

Along with his new Bahá'í friends, this young man had been involved for years, traveling from town to town in rural areas of his home state to share the Bahá'í teachings. We now look back with wonder at the excitement engendered by those efforts. This retrospective comment presents the range of emotions from thrill to dejection and disappointment. But that generation had tried something new that worked, except that there had been no follow-up:

> At that time in my community, ninety percent of the Bahá'ís I knew were diverse, very active college-educated

Americans, and we were fired up to serve what we felt was the real return of Jesus which we assumed the whole world would quickly accept to bring about the New Day promised in the Holy Books. However, the rest of the world, including a lot of the older Bahá'ís, were not as excited as the youth and slowly dragged the momentum down to a crawl by 1980. Moreover, by that time I had sacrificed pursuit of a sound career too long and had to be practical about life. So, like other youth who had made the 1970s a time of growth and high energy, we no longer had the time to do all of the work. Consequently, the growth and the excitement rapidly dissipated and the gains in numbers, assemblies and energy evaporated forever to be replaced by an intellectually, not spiritually based, cadre of people who had been spectators in the 1970s . . . Let me add that I am still pleased that I and a few others made those sacrifices for the right, the spiritual, reasons.

The mixing of generations, one of the signs that had attracted this generation initially, fostered deep and abiding relationships of mutual respect. Elders often showed great patience in helping younger, newer declarants study and learn Bahá'í writings:

> The small, humble community of Bahá'ís in my town were great teachers and helped foster my learning as a new Bahá'í, never criticizing my questions, never dismissing me. Many of the activities of the community, the deepenings and firesides, I suspect, were meant to help me learn, but were presented as beneficial to the whole community, which was just big enough to hold onto an Assembly. I feel fortunate to have found the Bahá'í Faith as a young person, while still forming my character and life habits.

This teacher, knowing it would be inappropriate to speak about his religion to his students in a public school, found ways to grab their attention and subtly share the existence of this new religion. And sensitive students were inspired to explore when exposed to such a teacher who found indirect ways to attract them to other spiritual ideas:

> I had a twelfth-grade English teacher who on the surface was teaching the Transcendental writers Emerson, Thoreau, et cetera, but in reality, was offering his students an opportunity to investigate who they were and what they were going to do with their lives. He didn't tell anyone he was a Bahá'í but folks knew he was special. He did this for several years. In each class he taught, there were always a few students who really caught on to what he was offering. Those few stayed in touch with him after high school. At one point, he told one person he was a Bahá'í and they might want to look into it. That information spread like wildfire throughout that group of former students and within a year and half, over fifty of us became Bahá'ís in the suburbs.

Learning the personalities of older Bahá'ís also revealed the kinds of tasks they'd been called upon to perform. This young believer thought she saw how a firm personality could be a boon in certain positions:

> Soon after declaring, I got a job that summer at the National Center. They were hiring more help because of all the new declarations, and my job in Membership and Records was to type up a card, a certificate and an address on an envelope. Though the job was boring, the community was thrilling. An elder believer on staff was the only person who dealt with covenant-breakers – and there were various pockets of them throughout the US at that time. She invited the ladies on the Center staff for tea and wanted to show off her talking parakeet. She balanced him on her finger and prompted, 'Pretty Perry! Pretty Perry' again and again. But Perry refused. We were all impressed when she lowered her voice and commanded, 'I WILL be obeyed!' Later we laughed about how this was the kind of character trait you'd need for dealing with covenant-breakers.

The older generation often gave supportive and wise counsel to their younger co-religionists, by showing them to look to the writings for guidance:

> A lady noticed my distress and told me the story of her and her husband having been ridiculed by Bahá'ís over a major business deal and their long walks discussing it. She showed me the line in the long healing prayer; 'I call on Thee O Thou Who slayest the Lovers, O God of Grace to the wicked!'⁷ It fortified my resolve that I could not be told to quit and must continue.

This young person was impressed by Amoz Gibson who had been elected to the first Universal House of Justice in 1963, and despite the brevity of his interaction, he hung on to a treasured memento:

> I still have a rose petal from the holy gardens that Amoz Gibson placed in my prayer book during the 1978 Summer Youth Project and for all participants. That still makes me feel warm inside.

Those who had the rare bounty of being around the Hands of the Cause were able to appreciate their various personal strengths. They were all believers from the first Bahá'í century and wouldn't live much longer, so this generation – though they may not have fully appreciated the Hands' actual accomplishments – was quite fortunate to have been able to meet so many of them:

> I met, though briefly, a number of Hands of the Cause who were universally strong but humble individuals. Only Rúḥíyyih Khánum stood out from them like a ferocious lioness, though I think that we generally felt we were too insignificant to approach them, which was a mistake given that we had worked so hard to make something actually happen at that time. Similarly, which is probably typical of

youth, I seldom approached any of the elders in the communities for their insights, because I felt that they had failed for so long to make anything happen, whereas at long last we, apparently being more aware of the Holy Spirit than they, were doing the work they had not sensed should and could be done.

Hand of the Cause Rúḥíyyih Khánum was of course especially dear because of her family's relationship both with 'Abdu'l-Bahá and Shoghi Effendi. She traveled and spoke frequently and never failed to impart useful insights. For example, in 1993 she's quoted as saying,

> We must never think there is a limitation on teaching the Bahá'í Faith or that there is a category that can do it better than other people, or some special system. Fundamentally, the greatest teaching aid is the Holy Spirit.[8]

The Hands were all so different from each other and their strengths were apparent. At least one of them would attend every large event or gathering, so it was possible for Bahá'ís all over the world to meet them in person. When they spoke about their relationships with the Guardian, they brought him to life for us:

> I was in a crowd where Enoch Olinga went down the line of people and hugged everyone, and saw and listened to the dynamic William Sears several times. Saw the very meek Mühlschlegel in Switzerland. I met Dr Muhajír who [gave me] some of the best advice I ever got. Saw Mr Furútan on my first Pilgrimage in 1970 who talked to four of us younger people about marriage. Received a letter back from Mr Faizi – I'd written him about his little book about the passing of Shoghi Effendi. Saw the last living Hand, Dr Varqá, on another Pilgrimage in 2006 . . . I loved listening to Rúḥíyyih Khánum, though she seemed a bit scary to some people. She attended the first international youth

conference in Europe, held in Switzerland in 1971. I was pioneering in Italy and was able to attend . . . The youth were singing a song whose only lyrics were 'Alláh-u-Abhá' and clapping along vigorously and this behavior angered her. She scolded the crowd, saying that we should know better because Europeans knew that clapping at church was disrespectful, although this wasn't necessarily the case among indigenous people of the world. It was definitely a needed lesson about ethnocentrism and reverence.

Shoghi Effendi had chosen the Hands because of the exemplary service they had exhibited. It was interesting to experience their very different personalities. And as inspiring as the Hands were, they were also human. William Sears was visibly rattled when a young man fell upon this group:

> I was one of a group listening to [Hand of the Cause William Sears] after one of his talks in the 1970s when a rather-disheveled young man rushed right up to him, ignoring all the rest of us, poured out a tale of his personal trials and woes, and asked Mr Sears what he should do. Bill Sears listened to the whole story, and [made it clear that the intruder's behavior was out of line.] Figuratively speaking, you could have heard the sound of jaws hitting the floor.

This man had close contact with several of the Hands of the Cause during his period of service working on electrical issues in buildings in the Holy Land:

> I was very oriented to the Hands. There were particular Hands I looked to for help and guidance and was fortunate that I received help and guidance with parenting, learning detachment and basic qualities, and always feeling safe because the Hands were always there to make things right and that the enemies of the faith weren't allowed to hurt us. We had a lot of cassette tapes from Bill Sears and the open letters from Bill Sears and I got to know him and speak

with him about marriage and children and patience with
the Bahá'ís and spiritual guidance and practical guidance.
When I worked in the Holy Land, <u>Kh</u>ánum was our boss
and I got to know her a little bit and she knew what was
going on with me.

Young Bahá'ís in the 1960s and early 1970s had the special
experience of meeting American Bahá'ís who'd seen 'Abdu'l-
Bahá in their childhood:

> An elder whose Bahá'í parents had taken her to see 'Abdu'l-
> Bahá when He came to our city was the one who deepened
> me with the 1960's booklet *On Becoming Bahá'í*. After a
> few months, she said the LSA wanted her to ask me to help
> her teach a deepening on the Tablets of the Divine Plan
> for the entire community – I guess that was because I was
> the only youth in the community at the time. Mind you, I
> was a brand-new Bahá'í but had ravenously read *Gleanings*,
> the *Íqán*, *Son of the Wolf*, *Hidden Words* and *Seven Valleys*.
> Reading my assigned chapters and preparing to teach them
> to others inspired me to go international pioneering six
> months later.

It's interesting how much is missed when you stereotype someone based on their appearance. Because this young man put
aside his prejudices, he was able to form a close friendship with
an elder who as a child had met 'Abdu'l-Bahá:

> Bill [Dorrida] told me that he counted his days as a Bahá'í
> from an event in 1912 . . . Towards the end of 'Abdu'l-
> Bahá's trip across the United States and Canada, He visited
> X, gave a talk at a Unitarian church, then gathered with the
> believers for a dinner . . . Young Bill Dorrida was at that
> dinner and met the Master . . . He told me that 'Abdu'l-
> Bahá appeared radiantly happy and 'giggled' throughout
> the meal. [I learned how] in those early days of the Faith
> in America, only a small fraction of the writings had been

translated into English, and the friends were greatly focused on what they knew of the Master's words and His living example . . . [Bill] remembered a time when every meeting began with all attending, each repeating the Greatest Name – 'Allah-u-Abhá' – ninety-five times before any other business was conducted. He also showed me an invaluable possession, a set of prayer beads that had belonged to 'Abdu'l-Bahá.[9]

Through some connections, this young man was able to host the Bahá'í author Stanwood Cobb, an early believer who had met with 'Abdu'l-Bahá five times between 1909 and 1913, who had been invited to speak at his college:

> I read his books and read about his life. It impacted me. The fact that he did write about his life . . . He could relate stories about 'Abdu'l-Bahá that I could understand.

The inter-generational tension works both ways. The time we live in and the pernicious effects of commercial media, imposing on viewers its own perspective of how they should be and act, aggravated generational differences. This individual admired several older Bahá'ís he was fortunate to have met, spent some time with and gotten to know what kind of people they were:

> I used to go to [Hand of the Cause] Mr Khadem's fireside. All of a sudden, a hush would fall over the room because Mr Khadem came in. You could feel his presence.

Other elders also set an example for youth who felt honored to have met them and regretful that they hadn't taken more advantage of their seasoned wisdom:

> In 1973 my teacher, who was a student of Pearl Easterbrooke, a long-time Bahá'í, was taught by Stanwood Cobb who had been taught by 'Abdu'l-Bahá, encouraged me to talk with her. She must have been in her 70s or later at that time,

and revealed a perceivable radiance – a spiritual light you actually had to shield your eyes from! – that was striking. I talked with her several hours. Looking back, incredibly, I didn't appreciate her wisdom, the subtlety of what she had said, though I never met anyone else who displayed that extraordinary radiance.

Some who lived in the vicinity of the Temple were hired to work at the Bahá'í National Office. They also had the opportunity to volunteer to guide in the House of Worship on weekends. In either case, they may have come to know some of the more experienced employees there:

> [I knew] the administrator of the temple . . . He had a way with people that very few people have. He was one of those people that even if you saw him from afar you could recognize the distinguished nature of him. If I had a choice between him staying on this earth and me, I'd gladly give it up.

Forming a close friendship with an elderly Bahá'í gave this already sensitive young man the occasion to show his friendship and concern. He was rewarded with new insights into the soul of his older friend:

> I stepped into Bill's hospital room one day and greeted him, but he didn't answer. His eyes were open and focused on the wall. Thinking he might be near sleep, I sat down and waited and was startled when he suddenly turned and said hello. He explained that he had been looking at the wall of painted cinder blocks and repeating the Greatest Name for each block . . . [He] was very weak and struggling to breathe. I held his hand and told him that the community was planning a welcome party for some newly-enrolled members. Shaking, he pulled his oxygen mask aside and managed a single word: 'Beautiful' . . . That night, he passed away. Sometime earlier, [he] had joked with me, saying, 'We Bahá'ís don't die; we ascend!'[10]

Bahá'u'lláh quotes an Islamic hadith, 'One hour's reflection is preferable to seventy years of pious worship.'[11] He also said, 'Immerse yourselves in the ocean of My words, that ye may unravel its secrets, and discover all the pearls of wisdom that lie hid in its depths.'[12] This young believer was excited to explore prayer for himself and learned to see it as a private individual matter.

> Having reached the point that I regularly said a daily prayer, and would even add one or two others from time to time, I was somewhat impressed with my spiritual development. So, I asked my [older] friend to tell me about prayer. [He] pointed to his bedside table and told me to hand him his prayer book. I noticed it was an older edition that I hadn't seen . . .
> Every day, I say all of the 'healing' prayers, and all of the 'forgiveness' prayers, and the 'teaching' prayers. I say the Tablet of Aḥmad, And, of course, the obligatory prayer. Then, on special occasions, I say the others. I say them out loud; Bahá'u'lláh says, to 'intone' the prayers.

Stories about older Bahá'ís often feature just the highlights of their exemplary service. But when you learn more about their lives of dedicated service you might discover some unimaginably tragic circumstances they faced:

> In our community was a meek elder who served on the LSA into her mid-90s, and was always elected secretary . . . During consultations, she'd listen closely and sometimes I thought she was in agreement but just as we were arriving at a consensus, she'd raise a viewpoint that shed a new light. At her funeral I learned from a sympathetic relative about her younger years. I don't remember all the details, but she'd become a Bahá'í in the '30s, to the displeasure of her family, one of whom was a nun. Before she joined the Faith she'd been engaged to be married. Her family felt disgraced, apparently, and had her committed to a psychiatric hospital

for two years, during which time, of course, her fiancé broke the engagement. She never married but pioneered and helped raise up a first National Spiritual Assembly in X [not named to respect her privacy] and with the rest of that NSA, she's in the photograph on the wall in the mansion of Bahjí.

This young man would travel a great deal, partly due to being in the navy, which afforded him the opportunity to meet all kinds of people. Here he seems to have been comparing himself with others whom he saw as spiritually superior. Eventually he found someone to whom he could pour out his heart and from whom he gained some wisdom.

> Cynthia Olson . . . was the Knight of Bahá'u'lláh to the Mariana Islands in 1954 and lived on Guam. Her husband Edgar made Swedish pancakes every Sunday morning after prayers. I wanted to leave the Bahá'í Faith because I knew I was not being a good Bahá'í. But my 'mistake' was going to her to discuss it and not just sending a letter stating I no longer wished to be a Bahá'í to National – the official process – then fading away from the Faith. She convinced me to be patient with myself and maybe go to the nine-day deepening, which I did and it lit a spark in me and I didn't leave the Faith.

Little did she know, but this girl's favorite teacher happened to be a Bahá'í. He first taught by example, which inspired her. Before long she had become interested in the things that interested him:

> I had a favorite teacher who was a Bahá'í. I loved to read – still do. I saw an interesting book – '*God Loves Laughter*' – in the teacher's briefcase and borrowed it. Loved it so much that I asked for more.

Some respondents felt that they had endured issues that have since been resolved. Individuals who had tried to create another version of the Bahá'í Faith – known as 'covenant-breakers' because they ignore Bahá'u'lláh's laws and guidance – have all but vanished. Most clergy and other faith leaders in the US don't directly attack the Faith as much now. Thus this veteran Bahá'í expresses his relief that younger people are stepping up and sharing the tasks which are necessary for creating a strong administrative order, just as his generation helped to pick up some of the load in the 1970s.

> Looking back, I do think that the old-timers were by the 1970s pretty worn out, having endured the attacks of the covenant-breakers and hostile clergy, so that, by that time, there were very few of them alive and active, and they were probably happy to see some new energy finally picking up where they had struggled so long and painfully to make the Faith modestly respected.

Indeed, it's amazing to think that we actually met the generation of older Bahá'ís who had met 'Abdu'l-Bahá when they were children. That's such a precious connection to the beginning not just of the Faith but also of the Faith in America. The following anecdote is of a woman who'd met 'Abdu'l-Bahá as well as Lua Getsinger:

> Our Bahá'í community . . . was blessed with the presence of Augusta Reagle, who had met 'Abdu'l-Bahá when she lived in Washington, D.C. as a young mother in 1911–1912. 'Gussie' was a dear soul, in her 90s by the time we met her . . . I can still hear her voice saying the Prayer for the Central States . . . Gussie told the story of sitting at the feet of 'Abdu'l-Bahá and feeling His abundant love. She told of a time when 'Abdu'l-Bahá was to give a talk, and she had to bring her four-year-old daughter along. She tried to sit in the back of the room, but 'Abdu'l-Bahá took her daughter by the hand and led her to the stage, where He placed her in a chair next to a tall vase of flowers, where she remained while He spoke. Gussie watched her daughter, worried that

she would reach out and knock over the vase, but she sat quietly throughout the talk. Afterward, Gussie asked her how she had managed to be so still, and her daughter said, "Abdu'l-Bahá put me there, so I had to stay put.'

Persian Bahá'í Refugees

The Faith in the United States grew from 10,000 in 1964 to 60,000 in 1973 and many of those new Bahá'ís were youth – the old-timers had to figure out how to incorporate us. But by 1978 the respondents, then largely in their 30s, had gained experience in building and administering communities.

The Iranian revolution in 1979 overthrew the Shah and installed an Islamic government headed by Ayatollah Khomeini, a cleric who declared Iran an Islamic republic while returning the country to one where conservative social values were enforced, such as removing the rights of women in marriage, patrolling the streets to enforce dress codes and punishing those whom they considered to be enemies of the state. Demonstrating their opposition to the United States, which had supported the Shah and had attempted to thwart the Iranian revolution, Iranians stormed the American embassy and held hostage 66 diplomats and citizens, 53 of them for 444 days.

As the Iranian revolution was happening, a huge number of Persian Bahá'ís sought refuge in the USA, made necessary by their increased persecution by the new regime. According to the Bahá'í National External Affairs Office (2009), about 13,000 Bahá'í refugees fled Iran because of religious persecution and settled in the United States. Overall, they increased the Bahá'í population in the US by 15 per cent.[13]

I asked respondents about their experiences of incorporating Persians into their communities. People where I lived during the first wave of immigrants hadn't been apprised that the Persians were beginning to settle in nearby Bahá'í communities.

Bahá'ís living in some parts of the United States welcomed substantial numbers of Persian immigrants who brought their customs with them. The 'baby-boom' generation that had overwhelmed the older Bahá'ís with their unfamiliar behaviors were themselves now challenged with a sudden influx of individuals with understandings and behaviors different from theirs. This led to many of the respondents having to take a new look at their own understanding of the Bahá'í teachings as well as to face their own prejudices.

In large metropolitan areas, there should have been at least a modicum of familiarity with living among people from other cultures. For Bahá'í communities, with the influx of large numbers of Iranians, the difference was that suddenly members of the community from both American and Persian cultures were meeting in each other's living rooms and being introduced to unfamiliar foods and a language they did not understand.

> Differences cause tests. It's a good thing to have different perspectives – they brought that. I felt some of them were very devoted Bahá'ís and some who said they were Bahá'ís really weren't, or if they were, they weren't deepened. Some were strong and some were mediocre. They brought their prejudices, things like the equality of men and women . . . [which] was sad, especially for the women refugees.

The first wave of Persian Bahá'ís were settled throughout the country, and had been asked to go to particular metropolitan areas – Baltimore–Washington D.C.; Plano, Texas; San Diego and Los Angeles, California; Bellingham, Washington; and a few others. A second wave came during the late 1990s as the Iranian government took steps to try to purge Bahá'ís from their country. Most in that wave were economic refugees, some of whose businesses had been overtaken in various ways.

In both waves, the stories of their persecution and their escape were tragic, courageous and inspiring. Where I lived, high school-aged kids had been sent ahead of their parents. They had stories of being strapped to the bellies of sheep, and spending time in refugee camps in Turkey while waiting for visas, of getting onto buses in the US and because they couldn't read English, went way out of the way to the wrong city. The history of brutal treatment of the early Bahá'ís by authorities in the 19th-century Persian empire had continued to some degree in the 20th century, recognized by the signs of a more repressive government.

One respondent who lived in one of the cities where a large number of refugees settled, had thought a great deal about Persian–American interactions:

> Surely, the two most different international cultures would be those of Iran and America. To Americans, the Persians seemed too emotional, even irrational and a bit fanatic and yet ironically egotistical only saved by their attraction to prayer and admiration for the Central Figures. At the same time, I suspect the Persians felt that Americans were dense, spiritually insensitive and focused on worldly, rather than spiritual, success and only intellectually appreciative of the Faith.

The history of brutal treatment of the early Bahá'ís by authorities in the 19th-century Persian empire had continued to some degree in the 20th century which showed the signs of the development of a more repressive government.

Some of the American Bahá'ís accepted a Persian interpretation of the reality of the Bahá'í customs out of respect for them, as they came from the cradle of the Faith. Others were skeptical about whether these ways were proper and were uncomfortable with these customs and challenged them:

> I remember two very annoying Naw-Rúz events. In one case, the advertised time was six p.m. with dinner to be served at six-thirty. For someone who'd fasted all day, I was usually starving by six and would get light-headed not too much after that. But the family said they had to wait until the highly honored Dr so-and-so arrived . . . I later learned that the Persians were following their rules and had been eating all day, so they weren't suffering at all. The other thing that happened was because the Americans didn't

know that the Persian Bahá'ís observed the first day of Naw-Rúz on different days. So having fasted all day, I arrived at the advertised time anticipating that dinner would be ready. Instead, it seemed like every single Persian wanted to chant lengthy prayers so after sitting through two of those, I went out to the car and ate up whatever meager snacks were in the glove compartment.

Up until the first wave of Persian refugees into Bahá'í communities, most US Bahá'ís had come primarily from Jewish and Christian backgrounds. It had taken time for early Bahá'ís from different religious denominations to establish a common ground of behaviors in their new faith. Cultural differences were apparent between the Americans and the Persian Bahá'ís who brought with them different behaviors for Bahá'í gatherings at Nineteen Day Feasts and holy day observances. One respondent noted that there were no two countries as different from each other than Iran and the United States. Some of us learned from the immigrants themselves explanations for why they did things as they did. For example, when praying, many of the new immigrants would put their feet flat on the floor. I was told that this practice derives from a Muslim custom of not allowing soles of your shoes to be seen because they might have picked up something offensive from the street, so we didn't see the Persians resting one foot on the opposite knee, for example. And during certain holy days they would want to stand and face 'Akká, Israel, where Bahá'u'lláh is entombed, which was an unfamiliar custom among American Bahá'ís. Because Bahá'u'lláh taught the lesson that despite human differences, we can and should unite together spiritually, Bahá'ís are motivated to put this lesson into practice. 'Abdu'l-Bahá says,

> Cleanse ye your eyes, so that ye behold no man as different from yourselves. See ye no strangers; rather see all men as friends, for love and unity come hard when ye fix your gaze on otherness. And in this new and wondrous age, the Holy Writings say that we must be at one with every people . . .[14]

Anticipating potential cross-cultural communication issues, the US Bahá'í National Center even created a film in 1979 called *The Feast*, which exaggerated some of the cultural traits of both Persians and Americans in an effort to spark conversation about their differences:

> I felt like the Bahá'ís prior to the influx of Persians were pretty laid back, and the Persians were not laid back. But I recognized that some of it was culture and some of it was persecution. I recognized it but the biggest challenge was that there were good well-known Persian Bahá'ís that brought some of the Muslim culture and they'd insisted on some things that weren't in the writings. I feel like the Persians showed us that we needed to learn to be a little more reverent. They were sort of superstitious about it and it sort of rubbed off. The language thing was a challenge. It was dealing with the cultural differences. Some were country folk who came in '79.

The Persian Bahá'í immigrants added another dimension to the Bahá'í community with their language, their approach to life, their cuisine and the reverence they displayed. This respondent expressed anger towards Iran and was impressed that the new immigrants appeared to be relatively unscathed by their oppression and the ordeals of fleeing their homeland.

> We had a [Persian] family who were very nice, far more devout than I thought I was. These people had suffered under the Iranian regime and their families had suffered and yet they believed whole-heartedly in the faith. That had to be a lesson.

Persian Bahá'ís who were able to do so fled the country. Having been denied civil rights, they became unable to obtain passports so some performed dramatic escapes. I lived in a community where a college age woman and her older brother said they had escaped across the border strapped to the bellies of sheep.

Many lost their jobs and their property, Bahá'í marriages were no longer legal, and Bahá'í youth were barred from higher education. The US population as a whole was angered by Iran's actions. For Bahá'ís the outrage was perhaps more intense because of the oppression of their Persian co-religionists, conditions that remain in effect to this day. The outrage is voiced by this respondent:

> When you see people who have come from [a country dominated by] stupidity and ignorance as far as nationalism goes, and they still had an abiding faith in humanity, it's pretty telling.

In the Bahá'í community, both cultures had to work to understand each other. For much of the history of this country, Americans have been accustomed to living among people from very different cultures but not necessarily visiting in each other's living rooms. In the early 1980s Persian and American Bahá'ís did not always know how to ask each other about particular behaviors or particular meanings. Differences between the Persian immigrants – many of whom didn't speak English – and Americans, both glaring and subtle, made us all need to learn how to listen, be sensitive and adjust:

> I came to realize the American and Persian Bahá'ís did not understand each other: the Americans thought the Persians were cloistered, unrealistic and unreliable, whereas the Persians thought the Americans were unspiritual, intellectual and materialistic. It should have been obvious to both groups that there was only one Exemplar, and He never exhibited any of those negative qualities. Fortunately, there were perceptive Persians and Americans who considered His example and were able to make it possible for the two communities to work together.

Sometimes people who had either been isolated or in large communities encountered the impact that an extended Persian family had on their small community:

In our community was a large extended Persian family, several of whom were on the local Assembly. If they were hosting an LSA meeting or a Feast, they might start a phone chain to inform everyone that the meeting or Feast was canceled for that evening. They also decreed that they didn't like potlucks and prefer to do all the cooking at 'potlucks' which was fine with me. Turns out they didn't like the mini-hotdogs someone always brought but I'm proud to share that they always complimented my cooking and baking.

Bahá'ís in the mid-20th century really tested the Bahá'í teaching of unity in diversity. The first generation Bahá'ís were encountering a diversity of ideas and behaviors among the large number of youth suddenly enrolling in the Faith. The US community later welcomed an influx of Persian immigrants who increased the Bahá'í population by 15 per cent.[15] The US Bahá'ís worked diligently to understand how to live in a culturally mixed community.

The only rituals in the Bahá'í Faith are the daily obligatory prayers, recitation of the Greatest Name 95 times daily, recitation of the prayer for the dead at burial and the simple marriage verse.

Persians who had grown up with Bahá'í parents and grandparents brought with them some customs which seemed to be cultural rather than specifically Bahá'í. Sometimes American Bahá'ís thought that because of the rich history of the Faith in the mid-19th century, these customs must surely be more authentic than the behaviors which many American Bahá'ís with Christian backgrounds had learned in churches.

> The Martyrdom of the Báb came round a very few days after we arrived, and I was on the small committee that planned an observance just for us students. The one Persian woman on the committee insisted that standing, facing the Qiblih, and reciting the Tablet of Visitation at one p.m. on July 9 was mandated in the writings. The non-Persians asked [of course] for a reference for this. To head off an

argument, I finally said, 'Well, maybe this is just something we don't have in English yet.' She agreed, and we moved on. One of the mentors for the program actually contacted the Research Department about this and shared their reply, which was that, while the Friends might of course wish to do this to show reverence, nowhere in the authoritative texts had they found anything that mandated this practice. So, yeah, culture clash of Persians thinking something they did as a matter of tradition was the 'Bahá'í' way of doing things and Westerners saying 'show me'. By the way, that observance was thrown together with one student saying she had brought candles and another saying she had a pretty shawl we could use as a table drape and so on, and this somewhat scattershot approach to creating a small, temporary sacred space led to the holy day observance I remember most fondly.

Some American Bahá'ís also observed how the newcomers would always put their feet flat on the floor before crossing their arms and chanting prayers. They also came to enjoy the 'ash' soup served at the regular monthly Nineteen Day Feasts, the traditional Persian 'haft-sin' table (a table decorated with seven traditional items) at Naw-Rúz (the Bahá'í new year), and were inspired by prayers chanted in the original language of Bahá'u'lláh and 'Abdu'l-Bahá.

> I also loved the Persians that came then, and felt like they were special, being able to read much original writings, and maybe being direct descendants of early believers. I was excited that more blacks were joining, as that showed such promise for the world coming together! We held youth meetings, sponsored by a sweet Persian lady, Gazaal . . . I felt much of the music they had been singing was rather staid and boring. There was possibly a slight struggle to incorporate more lively music into meetings. Fortunately, I played guitar, so I could lead!

In a succinct statement, this man points to some of the overarching problems of and solutions to cultural barriers:

> I was a follower of diversity before becoming a Bahá'í. So from the very beginning I tried to sit next to someone who didn't look like me at Feast. And was and still am disappointed by the occurrence of staying within one's ancestry which to me happens all too frequently.

The culture clashes were more apparent in areas where a preponderance of Persian Bahá'ís settled:

> Often, Feasts were conducted in English and translated into Persian. But there were so many Persian Bahá'ís in one county that one of the communities only had one English speaker and meetings were pretty much held in Persian. I was sometimes the only English speaker at a holy day event in my community. The readings were mostly Persian chanting. And during the social time, I was often excluded from the chitchat. If I asked for translations they'd say, 'Oh it's just a joke.' I'd have to leave as there was no point in staying.

Communicating across the two cultures was something that many Bahá'í communities learned as they were doing it:

> We were trying to understand a culture that was ancient and rich in traditions. We also had a bit of hero worship for the descendants of Iranian Bahá'ís, and would often try to emulate them, badly. I remember when my children were little, watching the women holding their children on their laps with their arms crossed over their little chests, guiding them to concentrate and be reverent. I just tried to keep mine from running around and felt like I was doing something wrong. In one community in the late '80s we tried to have Feasts with translators, because half the time we couldn't understand a thing, and the Persians were left out. We were trying hard to find the balance and I don't think we

did very well. For me, these were the results of being first, our nationality and after, being Bahá'í. We had very few models of cooperative living with others, so we fell back on what we knew and with which we were comfortable. After 50 years as a Bahá'í, I think I'm coming a tiny bit closer to understanding that the only 'norm' we have is Bahá'í law, and we have to help others to understand that difference.

I was on [a] LSA – there was me and X and seven of the X family who had no experience with the administration because they'd lived in the holy land, so it was interesting. They looked to me for how the Assembly should operate. I had very, very positive experiences, personally.

The mis-reading of non-verbal cues went both ways. In the following case, the misunderstanding wasn't just across cultures but also across generations, thus doubly complex to unravel:

X's parents were newly arrived to X from Iran. Mrs [his mother] was a formal and serious-minded woman, one of the first two women to serve on the Spiritual Assembly of Tehran. At the first Feast she attended . . . she pulled [her son] aside and tried to give him money. She said that she was so concerned that many of the Bahá'í youth were so poor that they had to attend the Feast bare-footed. She wanted to help them get shoes. He had to explain that it was a lifestyle choice, not a lack of money, that was involved.

There was another influx of economic refugees in 1998–9, some bringing tragic stories about how their farms were, for example, confiscated by a Muslim brother-in-law who had married the sister of a Bahá'í (she had converted to Islam) and had the legal right to take over the Bahá'í brother's property:

Some of them who settled in our community knew no English. I got some educational tools for teaching English to Persians and started a class where I gave simple homework.

The younger ones knew they needed English in order to get jobs. After three weeks of class, one of the older ones who consistently didn't do any homework, said something to me that had to be translated. It was, 'Why don't you learn Persian instead?'

Engagement

Century of Light comments here about some of the developments in the Faith carried out by youth during the decades starting with the first Nine Year Plan:

> No segment of the community made a more energetic or significant contribution to this dramatic process of growth than did Bahá'í youth. In their exploits during these crucial decades – as, indeed, throughout the entire history of the past one hundred and fifty years – one is reminded again and again that the great majority of the band of heroes who launched the Cause on its course in the middle years of the nineteenth century were all of them young people . . . As an international youth culture began to emerge in society during the late nineteen sixties and seventies, believers with talent in music, drama and the arts demonstrated something of what Shoghi Effendi had meant when he pointed out: 'That day will the Cause spread like wildfire when its spirit and teachings are presented on the stage or in art and literature . . .'[16]

Change was in the air, hopes ran high, young Bahá'ís' enthusiasm continued through the 1970s and 1980s, especially in rural areas that had never heard of the Bahá'í Faith.

> I was more engaged in the 70s [than the 60s]. Youth can move the world . . . that was US!

Of course, service involves sacrifices of time, energy and money. For many of this generation as youth, they put off finishing college and finding a career path as they pursued service. As we used to say, they were on fire:

> I was involved from 1970 forward, really all through the '70s, so much so that I really had to double my efforts to get a practical career going in computer science. I was very early on elected to the very young local spiritual assembly of the community of X which was primarily young students from [the local university] and thought of little else but the Faith and how I could best serve it during that decade.

Out of the 66 respondents in this study, four have served or are serving on national spiritual assemblies, several had been on area teaching committees, several had been assistants to the Auxiliary Board members, 13 had served or were still serving on local spiritual assemblies and there were international pioneers to Brazil, Cameroon, Central African Republic, Ecuador, Italy, Finland, Honduras, Japan (two different families), Niger, Russia, Switzerland, Tasmania, Ukraine and Democratic Republic of the Congo (formerly Zaire). Indeed, they spoke of their service with a strong spirit of optimism along with enthusiasm. 'Back then, I felt like the world, the whole social system, could be changed in just a few years.'

Some of the most audacious among these respondents were those who went international pioneering and never moved back to the States.

> I married a Bahá'í, we have been married fifty-two years. During the [first] Nine Year plan we went pioneering to X. We have been living [there] ever since.

Besides the difficult challenges, pioneering became a rich experience as well as memorable. Some individuals stayed at their posts for the better part of their lives:

> In 1975 and 1976 there was a general call for pioneers to settle in dozens of countries around the world, so I

submitted my name to the International Goals Committee in the spring of '76. Pioneering was in the back of my mind as soon as I had heard of this kind of service. I had always wanted to do something special with my life, and serving internationally had a great appeal.

Many if not most of my respondents were actively engaged during the past half century and have nurtured their children and even their grandchildren to become engaged:

> I have served on the Local Spiritual Assembly almost every year since I enrolled. For two years I was part of a community of two, and there were maybe two other years I wasn't on an LSA. I have attended conferences and District – later Unit – Conventions regularly, teaching children so often that I was once asked if I would ever attend without teaching. I was on the Bahá'í School Committee for a total of thirteen years. My husband became a Bahá'í when our daughter was two, and together we raised two children with deep commitment to the Faith. I have been on Pilgrimage twice, made two trips to visit our daughter when she served at the World Centre, and have taken two grandchildren to Haifa to celebrate their Age of Maturity, and will take my last grandchild next summer for the same reason.

Youth looked up to the examples of long-time Bahá'ís as people with a depth of experience and wisdom. Rúḥíyyih Khánum, for example, inspired the youth with stories of cultures she'd visited that were not ensnared in the materialistic culture of the United States and where leading a life of spiritual values was less challenging. Several House members had served as international pioneers as had the Hands. The International Goals committee asked this individual to go to Africa:

> So after a few months settling my affairs and making arrangements for the trip, off I went. That is not to say that I didn't have second thoughts. In fact, as soon as I accepted

the assignment, my mind was filled with second thoughts. After all, this was nothing like anything I had ever done before. But if I had listened to my doubts, I would have missed out on a forty-four-year adventure that made my life more spiritually rewarding than I could ever have hoped for if I had taken any other road in life. And I did a thousand and one things that I would never have done otherwise including traveling through remote rainforests and savannas, and meeting people of diverse cultures. I taught school, got married, raised a family in a land that I came to love while serving as part of a growing and maturing Bahá'í community. I also got the chance to write and produce a radio program on child education and family life and another program promoting religious, cultural and racial unity. I also had the opportunity to attend a number of international Bahá'í conventions. So many blessings that would never have come my way otherwise.

Shoghi Effendi said,

> It is hard for the friends to appreciate, when they are isolated in one of these goal territories, and see that they are making no progress in teaching others, are living in inhospitable climes for the most part, and are lonesome for Bahá'í companionship and activity, that they represent a force for good, that they are like a light-house of Bahá'u'lláh shining at a strategic point and casting its beam out into the darkness.[17]

This couple had found the Faith, a year later got married, had a baby and soon thereafter pioneered to Ecuador:

> While there, we assisted in various teaching efforts and were able to visit isolated believers in the Galapagos Islands. Unable to find employment, we returned to the US after six months and resumed our home front posts in X, where we remained for the next forty years. In 2016, we made the

decision to move to [a nearby city] with a non-functioning assembly due to lack of quorum.

This pioneer became so deep into the cultures of two different countries where he'd pioneered that he was elected to two different National Assemblies:

> Living in communities, from the '70s until now, I'd call what I'm doing social activism . . . I've pioneered multiple places . . . and have been on the NSA of Russia and Ukraine.

After this couple met in college, they learned about and entered the Faith together, married a year later and after graduating went home-front pioneering to a small city whose assembly was in jeopardy, with only five members. The husband was old enough to bring the number up to six, but they still needed three more Bahá'ís before Riḍván. The wife wouldn't be 21 until the following spring. They've served on Assemblies almost continually ever since:

> Amazingly, within the next few weeks, three more people enrolled in the Faith, and the Assembly was formed at Riḍván. Soon thereafter, one of the new enrollees moved away for a job opportunity, but by that time, I was old enough to serve, and was elected to fill the slot.

It's always inspiring to hear about dedicated couples who have served selflessly for more than half a century – so far. Service to the Bahá'í Faith seems to course through their veins:

> During more than fifty years as Bahá'ís, we have often served as Chairman or Secretary of the LSA, children's class teachers, assistants to Auxiliary Board Members and members of the . . . Bahá'í School Committee. We have always attended Feasts and Holy Days and participated in District/Unit Conventions and attended almost every session of our

regional Bahá'í school. [My husband] also served on the District Teaching Committee, as delegate to the National Convention, and facilitated a Bahá'í Youth Workshop for many years. I supported his work in these roles. Since retirement from full-time work in 2013, we have had the bounty of serving at the Bahá'í World Centre for numerous short-term periods and continue to assist remotely.

There were a lot of restrictions on Bahá'ís traveling internationally. We were told not to go to Muslim countries or communist ones. Women couldn't pioneer to places where it wasn't customary for single women to travel freely:

> At one point during [an extended European] trip, I ended up at a Bahá'í summer school in Austria, I think, where Dr Muhájir was the speaker. At the end of one of his talks, I asked him how we should decide if we should travel teach or pioneer or stay on the home front or go to another country. He looked closely at me and said, 'You, dear, must do them all.' And so I did . . . I went pioneering to Japan. I met my husband (a Japanese Bahá'í) and stayed in Japan for twenty years . . . I then had an offer to go to Tianjin, China to be the principal of a Bahá'í-inspired international school. Of course, I went. I worked with an amazing group of dedicated Bahá'ís and after a year returned briefly to Japan before taking a job in Pohnpei. I stayed there for two years and was then offered a job for one year back in Russia.

When this woman went to a country where the U.S. had been assigned to send pioneers, she was asked to go to a city that was an internal goal of that country:

> I pioneered to a city designated by the Guardian as a goal in a country designated by the House in the Nine Year plan, supporting myself on the bit of money I'd saved up. I was thrilled and honored when Hand of the Cause Dr Muhájir came to visit me and took me to breakfast. I'm grateful for

this advice he shared that helped me sustain a lot of difficult times in the Faith: 'Turn your enthusiasm into steadfastness.'

Service doesn't have to be grand. Often smaller gestures are significant. The US National Assembly asked Bahá'ís to move from larger communities to those that still needed a local assembly. When this man moved from a community with an Assembly into an area with scattered Bahá'ís, he found a lack of any organization:

> There were a lot of isolated Bahá'ís in [my] area, and I got all the county Bahá'ís together.

This generation recalls when the NSA emphasized the importance of establishing local assemblies and sometimes asked us to move across city lines to raise a new one. Bahá'ís often moved from larger communities to those that still needed a few more people to be able to form local assemblies:

> My husband and I are currently assistants to an Auxiliary Board member. This is probably because he's appointing people everywhere, and we constitute the entire Bahá'í community. It took me a long time to realize that Bahá'ís, when moving, didn't immediately ask, 'Where can my warm body be of service to the Faith?' because we always did. We helped raise our county's first LSA and then opened a new locality.

These days, Bahá'ís who move for personal or professional reasons don't seem to give much thought to the boundaries between Bahá'í jurisdictions but in the 1970s–80s, most Bahá'ís were aware of the need to form or strengthen local assemblies:

> As soon as I was a Bahá'í, I was always looking for ways to serve the Faith. It took a bit of time to learn how to speak to people about the Faith in ways that would engage their interest and appreciation. I photocopied flyers and posters

and put them everywhere around the [university] until you could hardly find a notice board that didn't have one. While working towards a master's degree . . . I [moved] to help form an Assembly, which was a goal of the LSA . . .

Much emphasis was placed on establishing and growing Local Assemblies and many of the respondents acted upon that need:

> I transferred to several different states and served on Baháʼí assemblies there until [retirement and then we] moved to X, also to help the Faith.

Also among the respondents, 14 mentioned they'd served on local assemblies, several as officers. Seven mentioned they'd been home-front pioneers. Although we aren't constrained to do this type of service, it is a marker of dedication and commitment. LSA members were trained that an Assembly member's role is to shepherd and inspire our communities to take initiative and not wait for others to do all the work:

> Maybe the easy thing is to say we were never un-engaged . . . we're a bunch of very small communities in the county where we currently live, and we tend to do Feasts and Holy Days collectively. I guess we've been the ones who have tried the hardest to make sure Feasts get observed, online if no other way! When National asked that we try to make a big deal of the one-hundredth anniversary of ʻAbduʼl-Baháʼs passing, I brought it up at Feast but basically got blown off by people saying, 'Let's just see what [a neighboring community] is doing and support that.' I didn't feel right about that, so the two of us booked a meeting room at the local library, unsure what we were going to do, and then asked everyone, 'If supporting a local event meant all you have to do is show up, would you support this?' It was a really successful event, with seventeen people – that's big for this area – including some non-Baháʼí friends. Since then, it's been a little easier to get people engaged.

The respondents, at the time of writing, are now in their sixties through eighties, and, remain as active as health and mobility allow:

> Bahá'ís do not stop working – we keep working. There's plenty that we can do. I'm trying to encourage others that . . . we need a lot of help.

It's not easy serving on an Assembly, but you can learn a great deal about decision-making, fact-finding, detachment and sacrifice:

> Serving on a local assembly is a huge bounty but it's also a sacrifice. I think everything you do for the Faith is a balance between bounty and sacrifice. It's been my experience that a number of people that I've known left the Faith because it was too much of a sacrifice or they found things that were more important. I think that if you devote yourself to the Faith, no sacrifice can be too great either for you or for the world. There has to be something in your life that is worth going forward for.

Many respondents have continued to serve for all these decades. When this respondent first heard about the Faith, he was in college full time, working 40 hours a week in a factory, was married with a pregnant wife. Even now in retirement, he has remained similarly active, taking on responsibilities in service to the Faith:

> [Local Bahá'ís] had just come back from that [conference] when I ran into X at [General Electric] working second shift and that's when I became introduced to the Faith. [The Faith] has been the principal activity except for working. I was on the first LSA here in X. When we moved to Y, I was on a committee, one of the teaching committees, moved to Z and I was on LSAs for fifty-two years. I was on LSAs except for nine months. We traveled to other communities

in [one state]. In [another state] we had campaigns going on. I've been an assistant for three or four years. And involved in teaching as we all were. We traveled to other communities in [one state]. In [another state] we had campaigns going on. What keeps me in the Faith: It's just who I am. I love the Faith so dearly. I'm absolutely convinced that it's the salvation of the world. Trying to change the world. People don't know me very long before they know I'm a Bahá'í.

Many today are unaware of all the specific details of work that had been done previously:

> During the five year plan, we had a goal of one Bahá'í in every county. I was on the District Teaching Committee then for about a three-month period and we reached that goal. People came in from all over the world to help us – some were assigned by the House of Justice. I made great friends, and a lot of miraculous things happened. The result was giving us experience and perspective on different kinds of different strata of society in how they embraced the Faith. It was very much a learning thing. Minorities – Hispanics, African Americans – were open to us visiting with them. And it brought spiritual growth for the Bahá'ís. I kind of have my eyes closed to the negative aspects of it. All things are from God, in that wrong there's a thousand rights. That's how I thought about the mass teaching work. I thought it brought the Faith to a new level. It was a plan of the NSA and the NTC.

There are so many different ways Bahá'ís can serve their communities as well as the greater community. Often, those who actually volunteer a lot can mentor others. These Bahá'ís learned in their youth the ethic of stepping up to serve, a quality that still inspires them:

> Since becoming a Bahá'í, I have served on LSAs with my Bahá'í husband, taught children's classes, sung in small

Bahá'í choirs, have been the Feast and Holy Days coordinator of our community, Bahá'í librarian, have been serving as an assistant to an Auxiliary Board Member and have been serving on an Area Teaching Committee, have participated in Ruhi study circles and have tutored.

Of course, everyone is different and Bahá'ís generally need to understand that we all must read our own realities and behave in ways that are genuine and make sense. Here's a woman who makes a point that undoubtedly resonates with others:

> In that time period, the big emphasis from the national and international bodies was 'teaching'. I found that to be very difficult with anyone I didn't know well.

With age comes experience. This is from a man who has been an active and dedicated member of the Bahá'í Faith since 1971, serving on Local Assemblies, actively sharing Bahá'í teachings, deepening and meditating. Reflecting on acquiring some wisdom is a logical outcome of that kind of dedication. He draws from his understanding of the writings of 'Abdu'l-Bahá:

> Fifty years ago some of the ten Bahá'í principles that Bahá'ís still use to teach the Faith were considered harbingers of communism, others were considered disruptive of a society based on popular prejudices, while others were considered merely idealistic and impractical. But now they are seen as insightful, socially overdue and, at least, interesting. The eleventh principle is the Holy Spirit which 'Abdu'l-Bahá often mentioned as the way to end hate and the only path to a trustworthy peace.[18]

'Abdu'l-Bahá also wrote,

> Know thou that all the powers combined have not the power to establish universal peace, nor to withstand the overmastering dominion, at every time and season, of these

endless wars. Ere long, however, shall the power of heaven, the dominion of the Holy Spirit, hoist on the high summits the banners of love and peace, and there above the castles of majesty and might shall those banners wave in the rushing winds that blow out of the tender mercy of God.[19]

Others realized during their youth that they had to balance service to the Faith with other responsibilities, including finding work which allowed them to live productive and effective lives which enabled them to contribute to society.

I graduated from college in early 1971 and came to believe the Faith was all that was important, that I could survive on low-paying jobs and spend the majority of my time involved in mass teaching efforts all over our state. As I approached age thirty, I realized such thinking was not realistic and managed to get a second and more practical degree that would give me a decent income for the rest of my life . . . Nevertheless, I had no doubt of the sincerity, dedication and spiritual awareness of the dozen or so of us that actually did run all over the state at that time. We were all very much aware of the Holy Spirit and felt that the people we enrolled were aware of It as well, though too few Bahá'ís supported them and most drifted away.

Too often such ways of the culture at large – though we know it's toxic – intrude into Bahá'í behavior, language and thought. This person is scrupulous even about the effects of word choice that others often don't notice. In American culture, positions and titles are often seen as prizes you must compete for, so people learn that such status means that you're an important person, ideas that Americans need to unlearn when they become Bahá'ís. Some individual differences aren't readily apparent. And in fact, our only real differences are in our thoughts, not in our appearances or behaviors. In diverse communities, people learn to be watchful of how they say things:

I was enthralled by the stories of older Bahá'ís and of those from other countries. It wasn't until I had been a Bahá'í for some years that I became troubled by the terms 'American Bahá'í' or 'Iranian Bahá'í' or 'Japanese Bahá'í'. My understanding had always been that we were trying to establish a new world order without these divisions or differences. I was trying to raise my children to be part or a new culture – the Bahá'í culture. It still disturbs me to hear these terms, but I have never brought it up in a group. I guess I have now . . .

Comparing his present-day experience with recollections from the past, one respondent perceived that the interpersonal help and attention he had received as a youth was in some ways stronger than that of the present:

> . . . we had youth and a variety of adults helping us along and getting us to take action.

The Bahá'í procedure for consultation is not the same as the ways in which decision-making occurs in the culture at large because it contains a spiritual component. Consultation is practiced throughout the Bahá'í community, always with the aim of finding the truth in all situations. In much of the western world, persuasion is a dominant characteristic of decision-making, as people use logical arguments in an attempt to convince others to see situations their way. 'Abdu'l-Bahá describes some of the aspects of consultation:

> The members thereof must take counsel together in such wise that no occasion for ill-feeling or discord may arise. This can be attained when every member expresseth with absolute freedom his own opinion and setteth forth his argument. Should anyone oppose, he must on no account feel hurt for not until matters are fully discussed can the right way be revealed. The shining spark of truth cometh forth only after the clash of differing opinions. If after

discussion, a decision be carried unanimously well and good; but if, the Lord forbid, differences of opinion should arise, a majority of voices must prevail.[20]

Bahá'ís are charged with personally praying, meditating and studying the Bahá'í writings in order to carry out their role as individual members of a community that relies on knowledgeable members who study the Bahá'í scripture every day. The following respondent's remarks show his frustration about – and perhaps impatience with – what he sees as a lack of individuals' understanding stemming from a lack of focus on the writings. While the Bahá'í teachings provide spiritual and practical guidance for decision-making and problem-solving through consultation, many individuals seem to be overly influenced by the ineffective approach of the dominant national culture:

> I have heard Bahá'ís who work as counselors say that some of their Bahá'í clients' marital problems stem from their inability to recognize and discuss the flaws in their relationships because neither party wants to admit to any shortcomings. The same might be said about institutions whose members respond to criticisms by saying, 'We're in a culture of learning' and change the subject. So some real painful situations don't get addressed. Bahá'u'lláh even says that backbiting can result in apathetic communities. I've been on LSAs in several different communities, two of which swept backbiting under the rug. They even called [Auxiliary Board members] for help but their advice has been the same – 'We should all just love each other.' Sorry, but that doesn't work.

The United States is among the most religiously diverse countries in the world whose society in general continues to be more understanding of and sympathetic towards differences in human behavior. Bahá'ís in this country are informed by society in general, which is probably true in most countries. Back in the mid-20th century, there was little or no awareness or understanding about how some individuals – including the individuals themselves – were neuroatypical and reacted differently from most to stimuli, a condition that's better understood today.

> I know that if I were an extrovert or shining personality, had a degree, car, speech, and stellar resume, that I could have given firesides in many large cities . . . Looks are everything! I never looked good. Independent, individual, introverted, not in a group activity, no job, homeless, no career, no family or marriage, and no desire or plan to get any of that. Nobody really wants their kids to talk to me because I will encourage them to follow their dreams and not just do what your parents did or the social norms of higher education, college, job, career, marriage, family, retire and die.

Here's a man who had a gentle way of encouraging Bahá'ís who expressed concerns that they might be carrying too much cultural baggage to fully engage in the Faith.

> I became an assistant for the Auxiliary Board member. I liked it because all I did was encourage people. People would get hung up carrying their culture into the Faith, and I felt it was a little overkill. Being an Assistant was a good way to encourage people to be moderate in their concerns about that sort of thing, and that we're doing the best we can. I always felt like I was doing my job. I felt that I was doing the right thing.

This is a clear-eyed view of the overall effects of working shoulder-to-shoulder to reform a world that is stuck in adolescent acting out:

> Since 1970 I have lived in numerous places, worked at the National Center for five years and served on many Assemblies. It has not been easy to remain a Bahá'í. I've had lots of tests but have stubbornly hung in there because this is the last great hope for the world.

Many Bahá'ís became involved in the community at large. This individual has been involved in social activism throughout his life, especially helping people in the greater community:

> Activists are very much anti-material – I didn't want to and never did live a material life. I wanted to serve, help societies and people who needed support.

Remaining Active

Remaining active in a religion with no clergy, where one's service is usually hidden and unacknowledged, is no small feat. This reality goes against strong cultural norms about how we need to draw attention to ourselves, be a 'squeaky wheel' that gets noticed, self-promote and market ourselves.

In the Bahá'í Faith everyone is called upon to serve in some capacity. If no one steps up to help with the work, nothing happens. There have been numerous areas where a ninth person didn't want to move across the boundary line to join the eight who needed one more to form an Assembly; there have been Assemblies that couldn't meet because they couldn't convene the five people needed to form a quorum. There have been Assemblies that never formulated plans because they thought their sole task was to read the monthly letter from the National Assembly and do what they asked. Rather, this is a Faith where everyone needs to voluntarily participate.

The respondents in this study have all remained actively engaged in the Bahá'í Faith for the past half century:

> What keeps me in the Faith? What keeps a fish in water? How else would it live? I found the very spiritual purpose of life through Bahá'u'lláh, so I cannot imagine another way to live.

Being connected to the Holy Spirit is the greatest lesson any of us can learn and internalize. This stalwart has continued for decades to focus on Bahá'u'lláh. Though Bahá'ís often overlook the term Holy Spirit, for this respondent it's the heart center of the Baháʼí Faith and indeed of all religion.

> My belief is that Baháʼuʼlláh is who He says He is, is why I've remained in the Faith.

Similarly, this individual describes his pilgrimage in the years before Baháʼuʼlláh's cell in ʻAkká had been renovated. At that time, there were no floor coverings, no glass on the windows and a pilgrim was able to get a small taste of the austere living conditions Baháʼuʼlláh had suffered through.

> My first pilgrimage was in 1976 and I remember going in there and thinking this is where they kept a Manifestation of God and I thought, how stupid are these people. Obviously, they didn't know or they didn't care who He was.

Building a bond with the Manifestation for today and maintaining it through humble and sincere prayer is perhaps the best way to remain firm:

> I am one of [those] people . . . who enter the Baháʼí Faith and grow and develop in it until achieving a level of certitude that is unassailable by inner doubts or outer opposition. This is the person who KNOWS that Baháʼuʼlláh is the True One and who can't imagine turning their back on Him.

Remaining steadfast in one's faith is really pretty simple, although we may become distracted and neglectful at times. Again, awareness of the Holy Spirit was mentioned. The respondents are still passionate about their beliefs and their Baháʼí affiliation, even after half a century or more, like this woman who is 'clinging to the cord':

> Remember I said if God wanted me to follow some other path, I trusted He would let me know? Well, it's been fifty years and no other message has been conveyed to me. The

beauty that the Faith offers to all mankind, whether it's gardens, or writings, or the actions of loved friends, all are parts of the attraction for me. *No* other beauty can surpass it.

The following quote is from a man who remembers moments when he wasn't sure he could continue to help do the work required of Bahá'ís which is similar to some of the functions which clergy are hired to perform in other religions, especially when serving on Assemblies, for example. But he understands the agreement he made in joining a religion that asks a great deal from its adherents and he remains committed:

> There were times – not lately – when I wondered, is this really necessary? But when you look around the world, what else is there that means anything? I didn't find anything that was so compelling that I would leave the Faith . . . the fact is that there's nothing out there that will bring about the things that Bahá'u'lláh promises.

By most or all accounts, remaining active is difficult. Service on Assemblies can sometimes feel like a thankless job, so when someone tells you they're on an Assembly, perhaps we should say, 'Thank you for your service':

> I'm now completing nineteen years of Assembly service in a small community, and every challenge delights me. What keeps me in the Bahá'í Faith? . . . it all comes down to one word: Truth. When I first read the opening of the Kitáb-i-Íqán in 1963, its truth devoured me whole. There was nothing else to be said or done. All its proofs, all its poetry, all its patterns, all its transformation of the world, took me up out of myself forever. No matter what happens to me, no matter what I say or do or choose, the Faith of Bahá'u'lláh is pure truth. Nothing would delight me more than to be dust trodden down by the feet of His loved ones. Still working on that.

Even some of the most active and dedicated Baháʼís face challenges, sometimes having to do with personalities or the actions of others but they manage to keep such issues in perspective:

> There have been times when I was disappointed in the actions of individual Baháʼís, but I have never lost my certitude about the Faith. In these times when there is so much chaos, confusion, hatred, and division in the world, I am grateful for the continued guidance of the Universal House of Justice. Having served at the World Centre and witnessed the heartfelt faith and sacrificial efforts of these wise and humble leaders, I can only thank Baháʼuʼlláh for this gift to mankind.

Steadfast Baháʼís understand the need to be of service to humanity, which is a primary function of religious teachings. This man describes some of the various approaches he practiced to get in touch with his inner self:

> I've also occasionally engaged in spiritual disciplines, for example, seated Buddhist meditation involving focus on breathing for at least twenty minutes. I've also engaged in what one might call 'extended prayer', where, after recitation of a prayer, I would sit in communion with the Beloved for ten to twenty minutes. As a result of all of this, there seems to have been the development of a modicum of spiritual perception, where I seem to 'feel' another dimension 'behind' the material dimensions we're familiar with. It's not that I can 'see' or 'hear' anything; but I seem to 'sense' a depth that I never noticed earlier in my life. One result is that I have more certitude about the spiritual world, about the next life, God, etc.

Educating our spiritual selves by immersing in the writings and staying connected to the Holy Spirit is of primary importance. This man teaches the same way he lives the Faith – daily prayer, reading, meditation and so on:

I feel that daily reading and prayer, and some type of spiritual discipline, as well as memorization of pertinent passages from the Creative Word, are all equally important for spiritual growth and for cultivating certitude; and one must pray for firmness in the Covenant. Daily reading of the Word and engaging in prayer are the essential food and drink for the soul. Though there have been, and still are, some who are illiterate, some of those souls have become lions in the Cause of God. But whether by listening or by reading, one must, as Bahá'u'lláh has commanded, daily immerse oneself in His Word, making It the foundation for one's spiritual life. As a corollary, this is why it is so important that, when we teach the Faith, that we don't merely dwell on sharing the principles – whether social or spiritual – but we must open the seekers' eyes to Who and What Bahá'u'lláh is, and help to knit their hearts to Him. And this is best done by sharing passages from the writings with them.

Here's a different angle on what keeps believers engaged in the Bahá'í Faith:

> It was pointed out at one time that each of us who is committed to the Faith feels a special connection to one of the Central Figures. I feel a connection to 'Abdu'l-Bahá. It is easy to feel that I know Him – all the stories told by those who lived with Him, visited Him, or met Him personally make Him very real to me. I feel I can strive to be like Him in some small way, and also feel the truth of the Faith, and if I deny, or pull away from that Truth, there is nowhere else to turn.

After filing away our rough edges over time, and doing the practices and disciplines Bahá'u'lláh calls for, one can arrive at a peaceful place:

> The longer I have been a Bahá'í, the more confirmations I have that it is the latest Revelation from God and the best means of solving the world's problems. At first my

rational mind raised questions and doubts, but I continued to study the Bahá'í writings and always found very satisfying answers.

It's bittersweet to look back over your life and notice aspects of situations that you hadn't recognized at the time, and reassess what you see as your past successes. Many respondents alluded to how much they miss the feeling of a community spirit they had felt in earlier decades. As this book is a historical record of individuals who experienced Bahá'í communities some 50 years ago, this sentiment merits more research and discussion and may be something that present-day American Bahá'ís might want to ponder and perhaps assess as they work on strengthening and deepening interpersonal ties.

> The Faith always gave me a family. I have found in the past decade that that atmosphere has waned. I don't see as many close communities anymore. Seems people are busier and don't have the time to spend with people. Teaching has become more formal and not as spontaneous as it was when I became a Bahá'í. My faith now keeps me in the Faith. But I miss my community and the 'family' we had.

This woman sums up her involvement in the Faith with a very simple response: 'Knowing who Bahá'u'lláh is keeps me in the Faith.' Others emphasized the power of the Holy Spirit.

> What has kept me in the Faith? Tangible awareness of the Holy Spirit. Not the membership or the elected and appointed leadership which is very human and very flawed as it is in every other human effort. The writings of Bahá'u'lláh, 'Abdu'l-Bahá and Shoghi Effendi are far more insightful and uplifting than those of any other person. So that for me the Holy Spirit, which the writings make easier to bring to mind, is the most convincing and powerful proof of the validity of faith in God, in this and in all of the inspired dispensations of His Prophets.

Here's a man who has thought deeply about how to remain firm in the Faith and seems to have concluded that reading the writings is all important. He referred to this quote:

> Recite ye the verses of God every morn and eventide. Whoso faileth to recite them hath not been faithful to the Covenant of God . . . Pride not yourselves on much reading of the verses or on a multitude of pious acts by night and day . . .[21]

He added, referring to another quote of Bahá'u'lláh,

> The world of existence came into being through the heat generated from the interaction between the active force and that which is its recipient. These two are the same, yet they are different. Thus doth the Great Announcement inform thee about this glorious structure.[22]

Finally, this respondent has pondered over the qualities of life that convince an individual to remain in the Bahá'í Faith:

The Faith becomes more wonderful every day. It is my belief that the active force is the word of God. Many believe it is the covenant but I have never been able to find [the active force] defined in the Writings. I don't believe it is but if it is, it's not translated . . . Following the laws is very important to keeping one in the Faith. The other thing is to read the Writings every morning and evening. When I became a Bahá'í, the Aqdas wasn't translated yet. I believe that you attract the Holy Spirit when you read the writings every morning and evening. I figured out that those who didn't stay in the Faith didn't do any reading, so I realized that you needed to do that. My wife and I started to do that as young Bahá'ís. Then when the Aqdas came out, it said to read the writings every morn and evening and not to do so is a big no-no, so if you didn't do that you are in peril. If you do that, you're more likely to be God-oriented, in your day and night and dreams. Bringing the power of the Holy Spirit. The word of God is the world of being. That makes being a Bahá'í more and more exciting every day, makes your dependence on God stronger and firmer. It completely causes you to be extremely firm in the cause. If you do that, you're ok.

5
Truth, Community, Service, Spirit

The more I studied the narratives, the more impressed I became by the intensity of the memories related by the respondents and the variety of their experiences on all levels, from their spiritual experiences to their acts of service. My observations align with those of the respondents as to the fear and worry in the country during the sixties and seventies, as well as the energy and optimism among youth and the awe and joy about discovering the Bahá'í Faith during those years. Having myself been Bahá'í since 1970 and having served several years on an Area Teaching Committee and 45 years on Assemblies in several different regions and as secretary as well as chair, I've always stayed current with news from the National Assembly and the Universal House of Justice, thus many of the activities alluded to in the responses are quite familiar to me.

I used well-known qualitative research procedures to analyze the narratives that were told in response to general prompts rather than as answers to specific questions. The process I used to boil down all the feelings and experiences expressed throughout the narrative was to look for common themes – that is, similar thoughts expressed throughout the responses, focusing on feelings rather than opinions – and continuing to sort and re-sort them into categories, leaving no major areas unaddressed. This chapter is my interpretation of all the comments overall.

As young seekers, the respondents clearly saw the folly of the Vietnam War and the evil of racism. The young women who weren't eligible for the draft had compassion for the men who were, and most felt for the young people on both sides who were being killed. But they could see that protesting helped unify anti-war demonstrators but also polarized those who disagreed. Similarly, all tried in their limited spheres to oppose racism. Many also shared a perception of their clergy's shallowness compared with religion's great potential. They understood – since childhood in many cases – that religions needed to be united inasmuch as they clearly shared common teachings. The respondents seem to have been detached in their seeking, even amid family and social opposition. Above all, they were inspired by the Holy Spirit. Their narratives indicate they were able to see with their own eyes and to judge fairly. In short, these are individuals who worked to be in touch with their inner selves and not to be overly concerned with what 'society' says. Maybe this is because they came of age at a time when the so-called great American experiment was wobbling and people were awakening to the fact that it had lost its moral compass.

Because the narratives reach back into the respondents' childhood and pre-adolescence, they afford a snapshot of both individual and collective spiritual development. The respondents as young people describe their ever-expanding communities starting with family, friends, school, the Faith and for some, the world.

I sifted through all the comments, looking for common themes. That is, I compared the sentiments being expressed about individual lived experiences, not focusing on their specific thoughts or judging the actions they reported. After looking closely at respondents' reports and sorting, re-sorting and re-grouping several times through their comments, four primary categories emerged that appear to dominate the collective responses: Truth, Community, Spirit and Service, all interacting on one another. It's interesting to explore how these themes work together.

Truth

As young people, the respondents were distressed about the state of the world – a war that directly affected their lives, violence against and killing of African Americans, and assassinations of men at the highest levels of leadership, both political and religious. But they also found joy in the music, dance and artistic expressions of the generation. Further, at some point in in their youth, the respondents wondered about reality, questioned commonly accepted knowledge, and had the courage to question even that which came from their parents and religious leaders. Further, they found ways to stand up to authorities who seemed blind to their own complicity, such as clergy who refused to accept the existence of other paths to God than the ones familiar to themselves. As youth, they sensed that it was only logical that any plan of a loving and just God would accommodate many paths and all people.

With spiritual tools at their service as Bahá'ís, respondents talk about their engagement with reading the writings, praying and meditating, all of which signify and deepen an interest in knowing the truth. Further, they mention friction with others with whom they disagreed as well as some personality conflicts but haven't allowed these to deter them from continuing to participate as they work towards finding the truth in any situation.

A fundamental Bahá'í belief is that all the Manifestations bring the same basic spiritual teachings but their social teachings are adapted to the times and places where the Manifestations appear. By the 19th century people on every continent were connected in some way, by explorers, merchants, invaders and migrants. In the first century CE even cities which we might consider neighbors had recognizable cultural differences. The concept of world unity would not have made sense back then. During the second century CE, Christianity had spread through the Mediterranean and Europe and early Christians were debating about which philosopher or historian should be listened to regarding what Jesus had intended. In the early years of second century Bahá'í Faith, Shoghi Effendi's plan was being carried out to establish Bahá'í communities across the planet so as to enable the Bahá'í world to elect a world body. And with the Guardian's passing leaving a void in his place, the Bahá'í community's loyalty to the Covenant has been tested, and triumphed.

Community

This is the most earth-bound of the four themes. Respondents provided numerous instances of their community involvement at many levels, such as their families, their friends and schoolmates as children and adolescents, neighbors, religious affiliations, towns, colleges and ever bigger circles. Their responses touch on their personal growth and social progress through interacting with others. They questioned the thinking in the larger community, specifically its support of waging war in foreign countries as well as its cowardice in opposing racial prejudice in the US itself. The respondents had learned to remain in touch with their inner spirit and perceive with their inner senses which were among the tools they used to evaluate cultural norms. Further, the descriptions they have presented reveal their pluck and determination as youth which enabled them to break away from the troubled world that had been presented to them.

When exploring the Faith, as well as after having embraced it, the respondents characterize the Bahá'í community as more diverse and thoughtful compared with other groups they were familiar with. They also describe the Bahá'í community as exciting as well as challenging. As Bahá'ís themselves, they needed to learn how to help perpetuate what they admired about the community, which often presented challenges. Because I'd asked the respondents to share their feelings and experiences and said that their identities wouldn't be revealed, they may have expressed with me things they wouldn't have shared openly.

During a period where this generation as youth were suspicious as well as dismissive of older people – there was even a popular motto that circulated: 'Don't trust anyone over 30' – respondents mention how much they admired the older Bahá'ís and loved hearing their stories about the earlier history of the Bahá'í Faith in America, such as how the Guardian sent messages to their communities.

The respondents express their awareness that the Bahá'í community is an evolving process and that a great deal rests on the shoulders of each and every individual Bahá'í. Community standards are to some degree negotiated in the Bahá'í community when believers worry about whether particular behaviors are consistent with the teachings.

The writings of Bahá'u'lláh, 'Abdu'l-Bahá and Shoghi Effendi contain many teachings about ways to properly approach decision-making and problem-solving, even among individuals The teachings also prescribe a unique process of establishing harmonious group decisions in consultation. However, in American culture people generally learn the skills of persuasion, which is a far cry from Bahá'í consultation. Because believers make a covenant to obey God's laws, community members may assume that they're all abiding by the same set of rules. But that doesn't mean they won't disagree. Teachings about interpersonal consultative problem-solving exist throughout the Bahá'í writings and are strikingly different from popular consultative approaches. To give an idea of some of the respondents' thinking, here are the sorts of ideas from the writings that may have inspired them:

> The purpose of consultation is to show that the views of several individuals are assuredly preferable to one man, even as the power of a number of men is of course greater than the power of one man. Thus consultation is acceptable in the presence of the Almighty, and hath been enjoined upon the believers, so that they may confer upon ordinary and personal matters, as well as on affairs which are general in nature and universal.[1]

> The heaven of divine wisdom is illumined with the two luminaries of consultation and compassion. Take ye counsel together in all matters, inasmuch as consultation is the lamp of guidance which leadeth the way, and is the bestower of understanding.[2]

When first encountering the Faith, the respondents were excited to find diverse groups of people who were enjoying each other's company. As Bahá'ís themselves, they needed to learn how to succeed in creating such a reality. For example, I personally was fascinated when I learned from several elder Bahá'ís their anecdotes of how the Guardian sent messages to the National Assembly which were then shared with their local communities. The House of Justice has picked up the baton and sends messages to encourage and inspire the worldwide Bahá'í community.

Respondents mentioned the cultural differences they'd been exposed to with the immigration of Persian Bahá'ís and how in some ways this challenged their understanding of certain fine points in the Bahá'í Faith. There's a Bahá'í teaching that says not to create rituals. There are only a few Bahá'í rituals: A daily obligatory prayers, the daily recitation of 'Alláh-u-Ahbá 95 times, reciting the prayer for the dead at a funeral and the simple marriage rite. Another point was to be watchful about letting any rituals to take root. The House of Justice wrote about this in a 1989 letter:

> Even though the Feast requires strict adherence to the threefold aspects in the sequence in which they have been defined, there is much room for variety in the total experience. For example, music may be introduced at various stages, including the devotional portion; 'Abdu'l-Bahá recommends that eloquent, uplifting talks be given; originality and variety in expressions of hospitality are possible; the quality and range of the consultation are critical to the spirit of the occasion. The effects of different cultures in all these respects are welcome factors which can lend the Feast a salutary diversity, representative of the unique characteristics of the various societies in which it is held and therefore conducive to the upliftment and enjoyment of its participants.[3]

The US National Spiritual Assembly sponsored the creation of a non-verbal film called 'The Feast'[4] which pokes fun in some of the ways the American and Persian cultures clashed with each other, each thinking the other's cultural practices were wrong. The film's main goal was to help the American Bahá'ís become aware of a Persian Bahá'í's point of view.

Fewer than 20 years into the second Bahá'í century, Bahá'ís were residing in 259 countries, islands and territories, and scripture had been gathered, safeguarded, catalogued, published and translated into 300 languages,[5] an indication of a worldwide Bahá'í community. In second century Christianity, scripture was still being filtered, assessed and disputed.

Service

Service involves sharing the teachings and helping to better the world in general. Many respondents were inspired to find ways to expand their circle, even by disrupting their own life plans and typical career paths in order to share the teachings they had embraced. Many of them courageously left the safety of the culture they knew and settled – sometimes forever – in a strange and challenging place where they were tested and forged.

Action comprises the choices we make – both worldly and selfless – and what we think about the choices made by others, for example, the decision to make war, to protest, to believe in God or not, to accept Bahá'u'lláh, accept or reject spiritual guidance and our social feelings about all that.

Respondents mentioned both large- and small-scale arenas where they've served or are serving on institutions including local and national assemblies, the Auxiliary Board, international and local pioneering, and participating in local initiatives.

Spirit

The overarching theme and most salient thread throughout the interviews is reliance on the Spirit, even before finding the Faith. Spirit runs through all the other themes. It comprises the deepest level of engagement among the Bahá'ís. In this category I include the love of God, power felt from the writings as well as from community be it family, neighborhood or Bahá'ís in one's area,

God's presence, spirit in the words, love for God, need for prayer. Spirit is our link with God. Spirit is like a circle encompassing community and action. Truth is the filler inside the circle. When the youth found the Faith, they joined the 'side' of spiritual unity and turned to uniting hearts, through peace and love.

Respondents were prompted by spirit, the catalyst for their initial search for truth, which inspired them to withstand social pressure – disdain, opposition, ridicule, ostracism – as they entered into and helped build up a refreshed religious community based on teachings. Spirit infuses the other three levels as it inspires and binds us together. We connect with and reflect spirit and thereby learn truth by staying connected to the source. This can motivate us to want to serve and in doing so the outcome is a stronger community. Healthy communities attract spirit and the process continues.

One way to remain spiritually healthy is to pray and meditate:

> My spiritual life and my Bahá'í life started out with BOTH prayer and reading – lots of reading – and this has continued throughout my life. I have repeatedly immersed myself in the most important works of the Manifestation that I had available: The Íqán, The Hidden Words, The Seven Valleys, Gleanings, et cetera. I've also memorized certain passages from the Creative Word which have provided important insights into and understanding of the profound verities which have served as an unassailable foundation for my spiritual life. Secondarily, I've read the most important doctrinal works of 'Abdu'l-Bahá – Some Answered Questions, The Will and Testament, etc.; and I've read the letters and books of Shoghi Effendi. Over my lifetime, I've also managed to read the holy books and sacred texts of other traditions: the Dhammapada, Tao Te Ching, the Gathas, parts of the Qur'án; even material on the Native American traditions. Throughout my life, I've always prayerfully immersed myself in the creative word of Bahá'u'lláh, every day, and pondered and reflected on its texts as well.

Even as young people, this cohort were thoughtful observers of the values of the culture around them, and could see many of the weaknesses, whether in government, their places of worship and even their families. They recognized the need to strengthen their local communities as well as the worldwide community and contributed to that by serving on assemblies, as pioneers, and in their own individual initiatives. They studied the writings, prayed and meditated and followed the laws – one even started fasting in the first week after he declared membership in the Faith. Most notably, they're attuned to their innermost feelings.

In contrast, we live in a world dominated by materialistic thinking. The materialist core of the United States prefers to dominate the world militarily to quell any opposition to its desire for material wealth and comfort. The nation's business owners and government leaders built wealth by dominating and marginalizing the indigenous population while eliminating them from their tribal territories, and using free forced labor of enslaved people in order to amass personal wealth. This is the animal nature in charge, with no unity, no peace, war, no spirit. War, conflict and competition are necessary in such a hierarchy game, with no desire or need for unity, but rather a desire for a stable pecking order.

> In the roughly fifty years that I've been a Bahá'í, I've perceived two kinds of people who are attracted to and then join the Faith. One type [tends to] . . . look at the Faith through materialist eyes, and hold its laws and principles as equally valid with the principles and ideals of the wider society; and if there's a conflict between the values of the Faith and society, they're as likely to side with society against the values of the Faith as they are to side with the Faith against society, depending on what their cherished personal beliefs and opinions happen to be. Some of these people, if they never advance into a deeper spiritual understanding of what the Bahá'í Faith is, often eventually find themselves in conflict with other Bahá'ís, and eventually become alienated

from their community and from the Faith itself, eventually meandering to the sidelines and into inactivity. Some come into conflict with the administration itself; some of whom even try to 'lobby' the administration to make changes they feel are necessary to 'reform' the Faith and/or its administration.

Bahá'u'lláh took power away from kings and ecclesiastics and devised an administrative order based on individual collaboration through spiritual connections among individuals who study and discuss the writings. This requires effort and not just remaining passive and thinking that others should do the work. Shoghi Effendi has said that the administrative order is a channel for the spirit.

> Should we build up the Administrative World Order to a point of absolute perfection but at the same time allow it to be hampered or disconnected from the channels within, through which channels the Holy Spirit of the Cause pours forth, we would have nothing more than a perfected body out of touch with and cut off from the finer promptings of the soul or spirit.[6]

Spiritual Forces

The four themes in the previous section – Truth, Community, Service and Spirit – can be seen as a continuum, or hierarchy, in the respondents' thinking. They begin as youngsters seeking for the truth about reality and come to recognize the power of a community of believers whose thoughts, feelings and beliefs align with their own. A foundational purpose of the community is to be of service to humanity in the greater world. And what binds the community together as well as serves as a personal guide to individuals is Spirit.

Returning to the theme of spiritual forces mentioned in the Introduction, Bahá'ís use the term to describe how change comes about. It's a term that needs unpacking. Just as the sun is the source of physical existence, the Word of God is the source of human life and civilization, considering that human reality is spiritual. 'Abdu'l-Bahá provides an analogy between the physical sun and the Word of God, and the Bahá'í writings explain that God communicates to humanity via the Manifestations. Bahá'u'lláh says,

> Verily, the Word of God is the Cause which hath preceded the contingent world – a world which is adorned with the splendours of the Ancient of Days, yet is being renewed and regenerated at all times.[7]

Bahá'u'lláh infused spirit into all creation, especially human consciousness which has the power to illumine our capacities and enable us to willfully transform each of our individual conscious realities. Bahá'ís consider the transformative power of the Word to possess spiritual forces that transform human values, leading to a God-inspired logic founded on the Word of God. Because, left to our own devices, humans largely rely on human thought and opinion that can ultimately lead to our extinction, such as derision of the very idea of God and ignorance of God's teachings while extolling materialistic ideas, we sorely need this spiritual renewal. As the Word of God enters deeper into human consciousness, it causes a reactionary response of resistance and opposition to change. The history of the Bahá'í Faith over the past 180 years reveals a great number of cataclysmic, ultimately positive, changes that have been resisted by strong human opposition.

Although people's actions and words are apparent, human thought is hidden. Bahá'u'lláh calls for the unity of humanity, equality of women and men, dismissal of clergy, and elimination of prejudice and warfare. Many of these ideas have spread throughout human consciousness amid great resistance by individuals holding the reins of human power. Such ideas are also hard to implement because of the entrenched ideologies that undermine them.

The Bahá'í writings explain that spiritual forces are the

foundation of reality, the fundamental basis of life. Throughout these writings you can find evidence that spirit or spirituality is not a mere dimension of human life but the motivating impulse of existence, without which nothing can live or move. 'Abdu'l-Bahá uses the image of the sun to illustrate this:

> Likewise in the spiritual realm of intelligence and idealism there must be a center of illumination, and that center is the everlasting, ever-shining Sun, the Word of God . . . Just as the phenomenal sun shines upon the material world producing life and growth, likewise, the spiritual or prophetic Sun confers illumination upon the human world of thought and intelligence, and unless it rose upon the horizon of human existence, the kingdom of man would become dark and extinguished.[8]

'Abdu'l-Bahá designates Love as the greatest spiritual force:

> Know thou of a certainty that Love is the secret of God's holy Dispensation, the manifestation of the All-Merciful, the fountain of spiritual outpourings. Love is heaven's kindly light, the Holy Spirit's eternal breath that vivifieth the human soul. Love is the cause of God's revelation unto man, the vital bond inherent, in accordance with the divine creation, in the realities of things. Love is the one means that ensureth true felicity both in this world and the next. Love is the light that guideth in darkness, the living link that uniteth God with man, that assureth the progress of every illumined soul. Love is the most great law that ruleth this mighty and heavenly cycle, the unique power that bindeth together the divers elements of this material world, the supreme magnetic force that directeth the movements of the spheres in the celestial realms. Love revealeth with unfailing and limitless power the mysteries latent in the universe. Love is the spirit of life unto the adorned body of mankind, the establisher of true civilization in this mortal world, and the shedder of imperishable glory upon every high-aiming race and nation.[9]

Hooper Dunbar summarizes,

> 'Abdu'l-Bahá describes the cohesive power in the universe and calls it love. It is the power holding the planets in their orbits – the cohesive force and connective tissue between everything. Love unites, composes and sustains all things. When love ceases to act on any thing, or if a thing moves itself out of the influence of that love, it becomes decomposed, disunited and discordant. 'Abdu'l-Bahá might have called this the power of unity, or the power of attraction, or divine energy; the name is not the point. Our understanding of spiritual forces is enhanced when we concentrate on trying to understand the systems and processes through which they function in the world.[10]

Afterword

Each time I sat down to work on this book and repeatedly read the respondents' comments, I felt like I was in the company of some of the finest and most reliable servants of the divine will who have remained faithful to their commitment these many years. What they felt and what has sustained them is none other than the Holy Spirit, though many have never thought about it enough to be able to define it. The Holy Spirit is not of the Creation, though it can be felt because it uplifts the innermost spirit self of each person who is able in private circumstances to turn towards divine attributes like kindness and love with an attitude of sincere humility. God is absolutely aware of the purity of our thoughts. By refining our thinking through prayer and meditation, we gain capacity to be able to sense the Holy Spirit.

While in Paris in 1911 'Abdu'l-Bahá explained the nature and power of the Holy Spirit:

> The Divine Reality is Unthinkable, Limitless, Eternal, Immortal and Invisible.
>
> The world of creation is bound by natural law, finite and mortal.
>
> The Infinite Reality cannot be said to ascend or descend. It is beyond the understanding of man, and cannot be described in terms which apply to the phenomenal sphere of the created world.
>
> Man, then, is in extreme need of the only Power by which he is able to receive help from the Divine Reality, that Power alone bringing him into contact with the Source of all life.
>
> An intermediary is needed to bring two extremes into

relation with each other. Riches and poverty, plenty and need: without an intermediary power there could be no relation between these pairs of opposites.

So we can say there must be a Mediator between God and Man, and this is none other than the Holy Spirit, which brings the created earth into relation with the 'Unthinkable One', the Divine Reality.

The Divine Reality may be likened to the sun and the Holy Spirit to the rays of the sun. As the rays of the sun bring the light and warmth of the sun to the earth, giving life to all created beings, so do the 'Manifestations' bring the power of the Holy Spirit from the Divine Sun of Reality to give light and life to the souls of men.

Behold, there is an intermediary necessary between the sun and the earth; the sun does not descend to the earth, neither does the earth ascend to the sun. This contact is made by the rays of the sun which bring light and warmth and heat.

The Holy Spirit is the Light from the Sun of Truth bringing, by its infinite power, life and illumination to all mankind, flooding all souls with Divine Radiance, conveying the blessings of God's Mercy to the whole world. The earth, without the medium of the warmth and light of the rays of the sun, could receive no benefits from the sun.

Likewise the Holy Spirit is the very cause of the life of man; without the Holy Spirit he would have no intellect, he would be unable to acquire his scientific knowledge by which his great influence over the rest of creation is gained. The illumination of the Holy Spirit gives to man the power of thought, and enables him to make discoveries by which he bends the laws of nature to his will.

The Holy Spirit it is which, through the mediation of the Prophets of God, teaches spiritual virtues to man and enables him to attain Eternal Life.

All these blessings are brought to man by the Holy Spirit; therefore we can understand that the Holy Spirit is the Intermediary between the Creator and the created. The light and heat of the sun cause the earth to be fruitful, and create life in all things that grow; and the Holy Spirit quickens the souls of men.

The two great apostles, St Peter and St John the Evangelist, were once simple, humble workmen, toiling for their daily bread. By the Power of the Holy Spirit their souls were illumined, and they received the eternal blessings of the Lord Christ.[1]

Glossary

'Abdu'l-Bahá ('Servant of Bahá'; 1844–1921): Eldest son of Bahá'u'lláh and His designated successor. He is the Center of the Covenant of Bahá'u'lláh to whom all were to turn for guidance after His father's passing. He is the authorized interpreter of the Bahá'í scripture and the perfect exemplar of His father's teachings. His passing is a holy day observed by Bahá'ís but they go to work and school on this day.

Adamic Cycle The period of time, approximately six thousand years, beginning with the revelation of Adam (considered a Manifestation of God) and ending with the Declaration of the Báb in 1844. The Adamic Cycle included a series of successive divine revelations which gave rise to the religions of Hinduism, Buddhism, Zoroastrianism, Judaism, Christianity and Islam. The current cycle is called the 'Bahá'í Cycle'.

Administrative Order The structure of Bahá'í institutions, conceived by Bahá'u'lláh, formally established by 'Abdu'l-Bahá in His Will and Testament, and expanded during the guardianship of Shoghi Effendi. Its 'twin pillars' are the Universal House of Justice and the Guardianship. The Bahá'í Administrative Order includes the local and national spiritual assemblies (in future to be called Houses of Justice) and the Universal House of Justice, the Guardianship and the institution of the Hands of the Cause.

Aghṣán Branches (of the Sacred Lote-Tree). The family of Bahá'u'lláh, specifically His sons and His descendants.

GLOSSARY

Alláh-u-Abhá (God is Most Glorious, God is All-Glorious). A form of the Greatest Name, used as a greeting among Bahá'ís. It replaced 'Alláh-u-Akbar' (God is Most Great), the greeting of Islam, during the years Bahá'u'lláh lived in Edirne. *See also* Greatest Name

Assembly *See* local spiritual assembly *and* national spiritual assembly.

Auxiliary Board Member/assistant An institution created by Shoghi Effendi in 1954 to assist the Hands of the Cause of God. In 1968 the Auxiliary Boards were placed under the direction of the Continental Boards of Counsellors, who appoint Auxiliary Board Members from among the Bahá'ís living in their geographical zone. Each zone has two Auxiliary Boards. The Protection Boards encourage believers to deepen their knowledge of and loyalty to the Covenant, and promote unity in Bahá'í communities, as well as protecting the Faith from attack by ill-wishers. The Propagation Boards promote teaching work, assist in the achievement of the goals of teaching plans and encourage contribution to the funds. The Auxiliary Board Members appoint Assistants and both work directly with individuals, groups and local spiritual assemblies. They do not make administrative decisions or judgments but offer advice and counsel.

Ayyám-i-Há (lit. Days of Há; i.e. the letter Há which in the abjad system has the numerical value of 5). Intercalary Days. The four, or in some years five, days before the last month of the Bahá'í year, which is the month of fasting. The celebration of Ayyám-i-Há is devoted to spiritual preparation for the fast, hospitality, feasting, charity and gift giving.

The Báb (lit. the Gate; 1819–1850). The title of Siyyid 'Alí-Muḥammad. He is a Manifestation of God, the Forerunner of Bahá'u'lláh and Prophet-Founder of the Bábí religion. His mission was to alert the people to the imminent advent of another

Manifestation, 'Him Whom God shall make manifest'. He attracted thousands of followers and the enmity of the Iranian clerics and government. About 20,000 of His followers were killed and He was executed by a firing squad of 750 rifles on 9 July 1850, along with a young follower. When the smoke cleared, the Báb was nowhere to be seen. He was located in the room He had occupied, finishing a conversation with His secretary. The commander of the regiment, Sam Khan, refused to fire a second time and another regiment had to be found. This time their bullets killed the Báb. His remains were hidden by His followers and in 1899 transferred to Palestine where in 1909 'Abdu'l-Bahá interred them in the sepulchre on Mount Carmel known as the Shrine of the Báb. The beginning of the Bahá'í Era is dated from the day of His declaration. The Declaration of the Báb, His birth and the day of His martyrdom are observed as Bahá'í Holy Days on which work is suspended.

Bábí A follower of the Báb; of or pertaining to His revelation.

Bahá'í A follower of Bahá'u'lláh. Of or pertaining to Bahá'u'lláh's revelation. The designation 'Bahá'í' began to be applied to the followers of Bahá'u'lláh during the later years of Bahá'u'lláh's exile in Edirne, Turkey.

Bahá'í community Refers to the worldwide body of followers of Bahá'u'lláh, to those in a particular continent or country and also to those in a particular local area.

Bahá'í Faith/Bahá'í Cause The religion founded by Bahá'u'lláh.

Bahá'u'lláh (lit. the Glory of God; 1817–1892) Title of Mírzá Ḥusayn-'Alí. He is the Manifestation of God for this era and founder of the Bahá'í Faith. Bahá'u'lláh suffered from the persecution waged against the Bábís at the time and was made to endure imprisonment and physical torture. He was imprisoned for four months in an underground prison in Tehran where He first received a revelation, through a dream of a Maid of

Heaven, that He was the one promised by the Báb. Bahá'u'lláh was released from prison but banished from Iran, going into exile with His family first to Baghdad, then to Istanbul, then to Edirne and finally to prison-city of 'Akká on the edge of the Ottoman Empire. While in Baghdad, on the eve of his further exile in April–May 1863, He went to a garden where over the period of 12 days He told His followers that He was the Promised One foretold by the Báb. While in exile in Edirne, He wrote to the world's kings and rulers of the earth, calling on them to establish world peace, justice and unity. In 'Akká, He was at first subjected to strict confinement for two years in the barracks. After moving from house to house within the prison city over many years, His jailors eventually allowed Him to move to a large house outside the city walls, where He passed away at the age of 74. Bahá'u'lláh's writings are considered by Bahá'ís to be revelation from God and more than 15,000 of His Tablets have so far been collected. His major works include The Most Holy Book (Kitáb-i-Aqdas), The Hidden Words, The Book of Certitude and His Tablets to the kings and rulers.

believers Term commonly used by Bahá'ís to refer to themselves.

Central Figures The Báb, Bahá'u'lláh and 'Abdu'l-Bahá.

Continental Board of Counsellors An institution created in 1968 by the Universal House of Justice as a means of developing 'the institution of the Hands of the Cause with a view to extension into the future of its appointed functions of protection and propagation', as the House had already indicated that it saw 'no way in which additional Hands of the Cause of God' could be appointed. The duties of the Counsellors include 'directing the Auxiliary Boards in their respective areas, consulting and collaborating with national spiritual assemblies and keeping the Hands of the Cause and the Universal House of Justice informed concerning the conditions of the Cause in their areas. Counsellors are appointed for terms of five years and function as Counsellors only when in the continent to which they have been appointed, unless directed otherwise.

Covenant/Center of the Covenant The instrument established by Bahá'u'lláh to protect the unity of the Bahá'í Faith. His explicit instructions were intended to assure the continuity of guidance following His passing. A line of succession, referred to as the Covenant, went from Bahá'u'lláh to His son 'Abdu'l-Bahá, and then from 'Abdu'l-Bahá to His grandson Shoghi Effendi and the Universal House of Justice, ordained by Bahá'u'lláh. A Bahá'í accepts the divine authority of the Báb and Bahá'u'lláh and of these appointed successors. In His will and testament, Bahá'u'lláh clearly appointed 'Abdu'l-Bahá as His successor, identifying Him as the one to whom all should turn after Bahá'u'lláh's passing. 'Abdu'l-Bahá is the Center of the Covenant.

covenant-breaker A Bahá'í who publicly denies the line of succession from Bahá'u'lláh, to 'Abdu'l-Bahá, to Shoghi Effendi and the Universal House of Justice; or who rebels against the Center of the Covenant and actively works to undermine the Covenant. The removal of a covenant-breaker from the religion requires the approval of the Universal House of Justice after investigation by the International Teaching Center and is a very rare occurrence.

declaration The statement of belief made by one who wishes to become a Bahá'í, including acceptance of the stations of Bahá'u'lláh as the Manifestation of God for this day, of the Báb as His Forerunner and of 'Abdu'l-Bahá as the Center of Bahá'u'lláh's Covenant and Perfect Exemplar of His Faith, as well as acceptance of all that they have revealed. The Universal House of Justice has stated that those who wish to declare need not know all the history, laws and principles of the Faith but in the process of declaring must catch the spark of faith and become basically informed about the Central Figures and their teachings.

declaration card A card, used by many countries in earlier days, to record the details of a person wishing to become a Baháʼí. It usually carried a statement signed by those becoming Baháʼís stating that they affirm their acceptance of Baháʼuʼlláh, the Báb and ʻAbduʼl-Bahá, their stations and their teachings.

Feast *See* Nineteen Day Feast

Fire Tablet A Tablet of Baháʼuʼlláh written in Arabic rhyming verse, revealed when great afflictions and sorrows surrounded Baháʼuʼlláh by the hostility and harmful actions of a few individuals who had claimed to be helpers of His Cause. Set out as a conversation between Baháʼuʼlláh and God, Baháʼuʼlláh pours out His heart in the Tablet and details His afflictions. God responds, ʻO Supreme Pen, We have heard Thy most sweet call in the eternal realmʼ and sets out the qualities that Baháʼuʼlláh has that will meet each of His difficulties. Baháʼuʼlláh affirms that He has heard the call of the ʻAll-Glorious Belovedʼ that ʻthe face of Baháʼ is ʻflaming with the heat of tribulation and with the fire of Thy shining wordʼ and that He has ʻrisen up in faithfulness at the place of sacrifice, looking toward Thy pleasureʼ. The Tablet is accepted by Baháʼís to be possessed of great powers and it is often recited at times of difficulties and suffering. Of this Tablet Baháʼuʼlláh states: ʻShould all the servants read and ponder this, there shall be kindled in their veins a fire that shall set aflame the worlds.ʼ

fireside A meeting held in oneʼs home for the purpose of sharing the Baháʼí Faith.

Formative Age Also called the Iron or Transitional Age, corresponding to the period since the passing of ʻAbduʼl-Bahá in 1921. This age is to ʻwitness the crystallization and shaping of the creative energiesʼ released by the Revelation of Baháʼuʼlláh. The Formative Age will see its ultimate flowering in the distant future in the Golden Age.

generation of the half-light People living today, that is, before the establishment of the World Commonwealth.

Greatest Name Shoghi Effendi wrote: 'The Greatest Name is the Name of Bahá'u'lláh. "Yá Bahá'u'l-Abhá" is an invocation meaning: "O Thou Glory of Glories!" "Alláh-u-Abhá" is a greeting which means: 'God the All-Glorious'. Both refer to Bahá'u'lláh. By Greatest Name is meant that Bahá'u'lláh has appeared in God's Greatest Name, in other words, that He is the supreme Manifestation of God.[1]
See also Alláh-u-Abhá

Guardian The Guardianship as an institution was anticipated in the Kitáb-i-Aqdas and formally stated in 'Abdu'l-Bahá's Will and Testament, in which He named Shoghi Effendi as 'the guardian of the Cause of God' and 'the expounder of the words of God', whose word was to be infallible and binding on all. His successor was to be appointed by him from his descendants. The Guardian was to act as sole interpreter of the Bahá'í Scriptures, while power to legislate on questions not mentioned in the Sacred Texts was given exclusively to the Universal House of Justice as whose permanent head he was to serve. When Shoghi Effendi died in 1957, however, the Universal House of Justice had not yet been elected.

The successor to the Guardian was to be his first-born son or another male member of the family of Bahá'u'lláh. However, Shoghi Effendi died without children and was unable to appoint a successor from among the members of Bahá'u'lláh's family as they had all broken the Covenant. In 1963 the Universal House of Justice sent the following cable to the Bahá'ís of the world: 'After prayerful and careful study of the Holy Texts bearing upon the question of the appointment of the successor to Shoghi Effendi as Guardian of the Cause of God, and after prolonged consultation . . . the Universal House of Justice finds, that there is no way to appoint or legislate to make it possible to appoint a second Guardian to succeed Shoghi Effendi.' Although there can be no new Guardians, the institution continues on, as the voluminous writings of Shoghi Effendi set a lasting standard of guidance for the future.

See also Shoghi Effendi

Hands of the Cause Individuals appointed first by Bahá'u'lláh, and later by Shoghi Effendi, who were charged with the specific duties of protecting and propagating the Faith. Bahá'u'lláh appointed four individuals to this position. 'Abdu'l-Bahá did not appoint any living Hands of the Cause, but did name four people as having been Hands of the Cause

'Abdu'l-Bahá developed the institution of the Hands of the Cause in His Will and Testament. One of the responsibilities of the Hands of the Cause is to protect the Faith from those wishing to harm it and to expel those who attack it. They were to assent 'to the choice of a successor to the guardian' and to elect nine from their number who would permanently undertake important services for the Cause of God. Shoghi Effendi named several people posthumously as Hands of the Cause and over six years appointed 32 living Hands. In the October 1957 letter appointing the final contingent, Shoghi Effendi referred to the Hands of the Cause as the 'Chief Stewards of Bahá'u'lláh's embryonic World Commonwealth'. It was this phrase that enabled the Hands of the Cause legally to take charge of the Bahá'í properties in the Holy Land after the sudden passing of Shoghi Effendi in November 1957. In the period between the passing of Shoghi Effendi in 1957 and the election of the Universal House of Justice in 1963, the Hands of the Cause directed the affairs of the Faith, pursued the goals of the Ten Year Crusade and called for the election of the Universal House of Justice, for which they decreed themselves ineligible. In November 1964 the Universal House of Justice announced: 'There is no way to appoint, or to legislate to make it possible to appoint, Hands of the Cause.' The functions of the institution of the Hands of the Cause were extended into the future by the creation in 1968 of the Continental Counsellors.

Holy Spirit The entity which acts as an intermediary between God and His Manifestations. It is similar to the rays of the sun by which energy is transmitted to the planets. The Holy Spirit manifested itself to the Founders of the great world religions and enabled them to reveal the teachings of God to humanity. In order for the Manifestation to convey to His followers that He was animated by the power of God, He has used symbolic language concerning the appearance of the Holy Spirit to Him. Thus Moses heard the voice of God through the Burning Bush, the Dove descended upon Jesus and Bahá'u'lláh refers to the Maid of Heaven proclaiming to Him His mission.

House of Worship (Mashriqu'l-Adhkár, lit. Dawning place of the praises, or remembrances, or mention of God). Generally used to refer to the central building within a complex of socially beneficial institutions such as a hospital, pharmacy, university, school and a traveler's hospice. The House of Worship is open to all for private worship and reflection and for public services. Only scripture of the Bahá'í Faith or other religions many be read or sung in the House of Worship. No musical instruments can be played inside and there are no sermons, lectures, weddings or funeral services, and no collections made. No pictures, statues or images may be displayed.

The first House of Worship, built in 1908 in 'Ishqábád (Ashgabat), in modern day Turkmenistan, was expropriated by the Soviet authorities in 1928, turned into an art gallery, damaged by an earthquake in 1948 and demolished in 1963. At present, there are eight 'continental' Houses of Worship, in Africa, Australia, Central America, North America, South America, Europe, India and the Pacific Ocean. There is one national House of Worship in Kinshasa, Democratic Republic of the Congo and a second one in Port Moresby, Papua New Guinea; and local ones in Battambang, Cambodia; Cauca Department, Colombia; Matunda Soy, Kenya; and Tanna, Vanuatu. Other national ones are in the planning stages in Brazil, Canada and Malawi; and local ones in Cameroon, India, Nepal and Zambia.

GLOSSARY

International Bahá'í Council An institution created by Shoghi Effendi in 1951 as the forerunner of the Universal House of Justice. It had three functions: to forge links with the authorities in the State of Israel, to assist Shoghi Effendi in the erection of the superstructure of the Shrine of the Báb, and to conduct negotiations related to matters of personal status with the civil authorities. Further functions were added later. The members of the first Council were appointed by Shoghi Effendi. After the passing of Shoghi Effendi, the Council was elected for the only time in 1961, the members serving until the election of the Universal House of Justice in 1963, when the Council was dissolved.

Kitáb-i-Aqdas (Most Holy Book) Bahá'u'lláh's book of laws, revealed in 'Akká in 1873. Written in Arabic, it sets out the laws and ordinances of Bahá'u'lláh's dispensation but is much more than 'a mere code of laws'. Shoghi Effendi described it as 'the Mother Book of His Dispensation', the 'Charter of His New World Order', and as the 'Charter of the future world civilization'.[2] In it Bahá'u'lláh sets forth the succession of 'Abdu'l-Bahá and His authority as Interpreter, anticipates the Guardianship and ordains the institution of the Universal House of Justice and its functions and revenues. He reveals laws, ordinances and exhortations concerning subjects including prayer, fasting, marriage, divorce, burial, wills and inheritance, pilgrimage, the Ḥuqúqu'lláh, the Bahá'í calendar, Feasts and holy days, the age of maturity, the obligation to work and its elevation to worship, obedience to government, and education. He also sets prohibitions, for example on the institution of priesthood and its practices including confession of sins; forbids slavery; condemns mendicancy, idleness, cruelty to animals, backbiting and calumny, gambling, the use of drugs and intoxicants; and outlines the punishment for certain crimes. The Aqdas also contains many exhortations to Bahá'u'lláh's followers as to the high standard of conduct they should follow in their individual lives and in carrying out their responsibilities towards family, society and their faith, as well as statements directed to the

201

rulers and peoples of the world. Bahá'u'lláh sets out the infallibility of the Manifestation of God and fixes the duration of His Dispensation at no less than a thousand years.

Knights of Bahá'u'lláh Title initially given by Shoghi Effendi to Bahá'ís who arose to open new territories to the Faith during the first year of the Ten Year Crusade and subsequently applied to those who first reached unopened territories at a later date.

Shoghi Effendi kept a Roll of Honour of all the Knights of Bahá'u'lláh. After his passing in 1957, those who moved to the as yet unopened territories were also given the title by the Universal House of Justice and appeared on the Roll of Honour. The final two locations, Mongolia and Sakhalin Island, received Knights of Bahá'u'lláh in 1988 and 1990 respectively. The Roll of Honour, naming 254 Knights and 121 localities, was deposited at the entrance door to the Shrine of Bahá'u'lláh on 28 May 1992, during the commemoration of the centenary of the ascension of Bahá'u'lláh.

Local Spiritual Assembly The local administrative body of the Bahá'í community. The nine members are directly elected from among the body of the believers in a community every Riḍván and serve for a period of one year. In some very large communities, a two-stage process of election is operated, similar to that for the election of national assemblies, by the election of delegates to a local convention. All adult believers in a given community are eligible for election to the local spiritual assembly. The assembly elects its own officers for the year and meets as often as it sees necessary. The local assembly oversees the teaching and other work of the Bahá'í community, conducts marriages and funerals, provides for the Bahá'í education of the children in its community, ensures the holding of the Bahá'í Holy Days and the Nineteen Day Feasts, and provides advice, guidance and assistance for those in difficulty. All its decisions are made after consultation. Bahá'u'lláh called for the creation of local spiritual assemblies in the Kitáb-i-Aqdas. The appellation 'local spiritual assembly' is temporary and will in future be 'local House of Justice'.

Manifestation The great Prophets of God, His chosen Messengers, who appear in each age to renew the teachings of God for the age in which they appear. The Manifestations of God are not God descended to earth, but are rather perfect reflections of His attributes, just as a mirror reflects the sun but is not the sun itself. They manifest different attributes of God relevant to the needs and circumstances of the age in which they appear. The Baháʼí writings identify several Manifestations, among them Abraham, Noah, Buddha, Zoroaster, Christ, Moses, Muhammad, the Báb and Baháʼuʼlláh. The Hindu figure of Krishna is also considered a Manifestation, although not much is known about Him. Baháʼuʼlláh mentions other Prophets and Baháʼís believe there have been others but there is no record of their names.

Baháʼuʼlláh has stated that another Manifestation will not arise before the lapse of at least a thousand years.

Messengers Another term for the Manifestations of God.

Mother Temple The first Baháʼí House of Worship to be built in a particular geographical area. For example, the Temple in Wilmette, Illinois, USA, is the 'Mother Temple of the West' and the one near Frankfurt, Germany, is the 'Mother Temple of Europe'.

National Spiritual Assembly The national administrative body of the Baháʼí Faith in each country. ʻAbduʼl-Bahá in His Will and Testament wrote: 'in all countries a secondary House of Justice must be instituted, and these secondary Houses of Justice must elect the members of the Universal one.' The secondary House of Justice is for the present called the national spiritual assembly and is elected when there are sufficient local spiritual assemblies in a country to merit one. Its responsibilities include channelling the community's financial resources, fostering the growth and vibrancy of the national Baháʼí community, supervising the affairs of the community including its social and economic development activities and its properties, overseeing relations with government, resolving questions from individuals and local spiritual assemblies, and strengthening the participation of the Baháʼí community in the life of society at the national level. The nine members of each national spiritual assembly are the electors of the Universal House of Justice every five years. The national spiritual assembly itself is annually elected, following the basic Baháʼí electoral procedures: no nominations are permitted, campaigning is forbidden, secret ballots are used, electors are asked to give consideration to moral character and practical ability, and those women and men who receive the most votes are elected. While the local spiritual assembly is elected by all adult members of the local Baháʼí community, the national spiritual assembly is elected by delegates, who were elected in district or 'unit' conventions. Each year, the delegates assemble at national convention, consult and share insights about the progress of the Baháʼí community, and vote for the members of the national spiritual assembly. In 2023 there were over 170 national spiritual assemblies.

New World Order The system of administration and governance Baháʼuʼlláh envisages in the Kitáb-i-Aqdas as revolutionizing the life of humanity and for which He has provided laws and principles to govern its operation. The features of the new World Order are set out in the writings of Baháʼuʼlláh and ʻAbduʼl-Bahá and in the letters of Shoghi Effendi and the Universal House of Justice. The institutions of the present-day Baháʼí Administrative Order constitute the 'structural basis' of Baháʼuʼlláh's World Order and over time will mature and evolve into the Baháʼí World Commonwealth.

Nine Year Plan (1964–73) The first of a series of plans for the promotion, growth, development and spread of the Baháʼí Faith initiated by the Universal House of Justice at Riḍván one year after its establishment in 1963. ʻAbduʼl-Bahá had foreseen 'a series of plans to be launched by the Universal House of Justice, extending over "successive epochs of both the Formative and Golden Ages of the Faith"'. The focus of the plan was a 'huge expansion of the Cause of God and universal participation by all believers in the life of that Cause'. The elements of the plan included publishing a synopsis of the Kitáb-i-Aqdas, development of the institutions of the Hands of the Cause, further developing the relations with the United Nations, opening 70 new territories to the Faith, raising the number of national spiritual assemblies to 108; increasing the number of local spiritual assemblies to over 13,700, building two more Houses of Worship, one in Asia and one in Latin America; the translation of literature into 133 more languages and a vast increase in the financial resources of the Faith, among many other goals.³

Nineteen Day Feast The principal gathering of Bahá'ís of a particular locality. The Feast is, ideally, held on the first day of every Bahá'í month, and brings together the members of the Bahá'í community for worship, consultation and fellowship. The program for each Feast is divided into three parts to correspond to these purposes. The devotional portion of the Feast consists of reading primarily from the writings of Bahá'u'lláh, the Báb and 'Abdu'l-Bahá. The purpose of the consultative portion of the Feast is to enable individual believers to consult together about matters of concern to the community, to make plans and to offer suggestions to the local assembly, the national spiritual assembly and the Universal House of Justice. The social portion of the Feast consists in the serving of refreshments and fellowship. Attendance at the Feast is not obligatory but very important. In general, only Bahá'ís are permitted to attend the Nineteen Day Feast.

pioneer A Bahá'í who leaves his home to journey to another area for the purpose of teaching the Bahá'í Faith. Many pioneers move to and settle in countries foreign to them, while those who settle in locations in their own countries that are designated as requiring pioneers are termed 'home front pioneers'. They are not missionaries but live among the people as they would anywhere, earning a living, sending their children to school and introducing the Bahá'í Faith to neighbors and friends. No special training is required for a pioneer although today it is helpful if the pioneers have experience of serving in neighborhoods where the Faith is developing vibrant communities of local people.

Plans Organized campaigns, local, national or international in their scope, in which Bahá'ís are encouraged to develop certain aspects of Bahá'í community life, take the Bahá'í message to particular areas, and translate the Bahá'í literature into various languages. All such teaching plans are based on, and are supplementary to, the Divine Plan outlined by 'Abdu'l-Bahá in His Tablets of the Divine Plan. The first plan was developed by Shoghi Effendi for the North American Bahá'ís. Called the First Seven Year Plan (1937–44), it had three elements: to complete the exterior ornamentation of the Wilmette House of Worship, to establish one local spiritual assembly in every state of the United States and every province of Canada, and to create one center in each Latin American republic. After the inauguration of the first Seven Year Plan, plans were developed in various parts of the world at different times.

See also Ten Year Crusade

principles of the Faith Term used for those fundamental tenets of Bahá'í social teaching excerpted from the writings of Bahá'u'lláh and expounded by 'Abdu'l-Bahá during His talks in Europe and America in 1911–12. These include the oneness of humankind; the common foundation of all religions; religion's obligation to be the cause of unity and harmony; the protection and guidance of the Holy Spirit; the harmony of religion with science and reason; the non-interference of religion with politics; the unfettered search for, and independent investigation of, truth; the establishment of justice; the equality of women and men; the equality of all people before the law; the elimination of all kinds of prejudice; the elimination of the extremes of wealth and poverty; world peace; world government; a universal auxiliary language; an international tribunal; universal education; and a spiritual solution to economic problems. These principles, 'Abdu'l-Bahá said, 'embody the divine spirit of the age and are applicable to this period of maturity in the life of the human world'.[4]

progressive revelation The concept that divine revelation is not final, but continuing. The concept of progressive revelation is founded on the belief that all the Greater Prophets of the past were Manifestations of God who appeared in different ages with teachings appropriate to the needs of the time. With each succeeding revelation social evolution has advanced, as the scope of man's sense of loyalty to a group has become wider – family to the clan, tribe, city-state, nation and ultimately to the recognition of the oneness of humankind, the distinguishing feature of the revelation of Bahá'u'lláh. Bahá'ís believe the great religions of the past were all different stages in the history and evolution of the one religion of God, 'eternal in the past, eternal in the future',[5] and that in not less than a thousand years, another Manifestation will appear, to bring further divine guidance to humanity.

Promised One He who is promised by the religions of the past in their scripture; Bahá'u'lláh.

Revelation/revelators The laws, teachings or message of God transmitted through each of His Manifestations to humanity.

Revelation of Bahá'u'lláh The writings of Bahá'u'lláh and His recorded sayings. Sometimes used to refer to the Bahá'í Faith and the dispensation of Bahá'u'lláh.

Ruhi study circles One element of the global process of learning in which Bahá'ís everywhere are engaged that is helping to build their capacity to apply the teachings of Bahá'u'lláh to the transformation of society. Using materials developed by the Ruhi Institute in Columbia, study circles are groups of Bahá'ís and their friends who study together to enhance their capacity to serve humanity. Initiated in the mid-1990s.

second century/second-century Bahá'ís The second Bahá'í century began in 1944, one hundred years after the declaration of the Báb's mission. Second-century Bahá'ís are those who became Bahá'ís after 1944. In the present book, they are individuals not born into Baha'i families who joined the Bahá'í Faith during the first plan of the first Universal House of Justice, 1963–72.

Shoghi Effendi (1897–1957) The Guardian of the Bahá'í Faith, the son of the eldest daughter of 'Abdu'l-Bahá and her husband, a relative of the Báb. He was educated at the American University at Beirut and Balliol College, Oxford. While at Oxford, Shoghi Effendi was informed of the passing of 'Abdu'l-Bahá and hurried back to Haifa, where he learned that he had been appointed Guardian of the Cause of God in 'Abdu'l-Bahá's Will and Testament, the expounder of the words of God and the one to whom all the Bahá'ís were to turn. He married Mary Maxwell, Amatu'l-Bahá Rúḥíyyih Khánum, in 1937. Among the achievements of his ministry, the following stand out as the most notable: the establishment of the Administrative Order of the Bahá'í Faith; the spread of the Faith to all parts of the globe in a series of organized plans; the elaboration of many aspects of the Faith and the guidance of the world Bahá'í community through the writing of numerous letters; the defense of the Faith from the actions of the Covenant-breakers; the translation of numerous passages from the writings of Bahá'u'lláh; the writing of books such as *God Passes By* and the translation of *Nabíl's Narrative*; the acquisition of land and the planning and supervision of the laying out of the Bahá'í gardens in the Haifa-'Akká area; and the supervision of the building of the Shrine of the Báb and the International Archives building. Shoghi Effendi passed away on 4 November 1957 while in London and is buried in the New Southgate Cemetery there.

See also Guardian

Supreme Concourse Also 'Concourse on High', 'Celestial Concourse'. Terms for the gathering of God's prophets and holy souls in the next world or spiritual realm.

Tablet Divinely revealed scripture. Originally, the tables, or tablets, of the Law brought down from Mount Sinai by Moses. In Bahá'í scripture the term is used for certain writings revealed by Bahá'u'lláh and 'Abdu'l-Bahá, including their letters written to individuals or communities of Bahá'ís.

Tablet of Visitation Nabíl-i-A'ẓam was a trusted follower of Bahá'u'lláh and was inconsolable when He passed away. He was chosen by 'Abdu'l-Bahá to select from the writings of Bahá'u'lláh passages to constitute the text of the Tablet of Visitation. This Tablet is recited in the Shrines of Bahá'u'lláh and of the Báb, and at commemorations of the passing of Bahá'u'lláh and the martyrdom of the Báb.

teach/teacher Sharing the Bahá'í message with others. Bahá'ís are enjoined to teach their Faith with kindness and goodwill. 'Abdu'l-Bahá describes the qualities a Bahá'í teacher must possess: 'Be a sign of love, a manifestation of mercy, a fountain of tenderness, kind-hearted, good to all and gentle to the servants of God, and especially to those who bear no relation to thee, both men and women.'[6]

Temple *see* House of Worship

Ten Year Crusade Ten-year teaching Plan initiated by Shoghi Effendi in 1953 and culminating at Riḍván 1963 with the election of the Universal House of Justice. Shoghi Effendi passed away before the midpoint of the Plan, and the remaining work was supervised and coordinated by the Hands of the Cause. The four-fold objectives of the Crusade were: the development of the institutions at the World Centre; the consolidation of the communities of the participating national spiritual assemblies;

the consolidation of all territories already opened to the Faith; and the opening of the main unopened territories.

See also Plans

Universal House of Justice Supreme administrative body of the Bahá'í Faith, ordained by Bahá'u'lláh in the Kitáb-i-Aqdas. Its membership is confined to men, at present fixed at nine. The Universal House of Justice is elected every five years by the members of the national spiritual assemblies who gather at an International Convention for the purpose. The Universal House of Justice is infallible. In His Will and Testament 'Abdu'l-Bahá states that the Universal House of Justice, with the Guardian, is 'under the care and protection of the Abhá Beauty [Bahá'u'lláh], under the shelter and unerring guidance of His Holiness, the Exalted One [the Báb] . . . Whatsoever they decide is of God. Whoso obeyeth him not, neither obeyeth them, hath not obeyed God; whoso rebelleth against him and against them hath rebelled against God; whoso opposeth him hath opposed God; whoso contendeth with them hath contended with God . . .' The Universal House of Justice is the 'source of all good and freed from all error'. Everything which is not expressly recorded in the writings 'must be referred to the Universal House of Justice. That which this body, whether unanimously or by majority doth carry, that is verily the Truth and the Purpose of God Himself.' The Universal House of Justice has 'power to enact laws that are not expressly recorded in the Book' and 'power to repeal the same . . . The House of Justice is both the initiator and the abrogator of its own laws.'[7] The Universal House of Justice was elected for the first time in 1963.

World Commonwealth A world community of nations governed by a world federation to which all national governments will be accountable: 'The unity of the human race, as envisaged by Bahá'u'lláh, implies the establishment of a world commonwealth in which all nations, races, creeds and classes are closely and permanently united, and in which the autonomy of its state members and the personal freedom and initiative of the individuals that compose them are definitely and completely safeguarded.' Some of the features of the world commonwealth are envisaged to be a 'world legislature, whose members will, as the trustees of the whole of mankind, ultimately control the entire resources of all the component nations, and will enact such laws as shall be required to regulate the life, satisfy the needs and adjust the relationships of all races and peoples. A world executive, backed by an international Force, will carry out the decisions arrived at, and apply the laws enacted by, this world legislature, and will safeguard the organic unity of the whole commonwealth. A world tribunal will adjudicate and deliver its compulsory and final verdict in all and any disputes that may arise between the various elements constituting this universal system.'[8]

writings A term applied generally to the scripture of Bahá'u'lláh and the Báb, the Tablets and letters of 'Abdu'l-Bahá, and to the missives and letters of Shoghi Effendi.

Bibliography

'Abdu'l-Bahá. *Paris Talks*. Wilmette, IL: Bahá'í Publishing Trust, 1972. https://www.bahai.org/library/authoritative-texts/abdul-baha/paris-talks/
— *Promulgation of Universal Peace*. Wilmette, IL: Bahá'í Publishing Trust, 1982. https://www.bahai.org/library/authoritative-texts/abdul-baha/promulgation-universal-peace/
— *Selections from the Writings of 'Abdu'l-Bahá*. Haifa: Bahá'í World Centre, 1978. https://www.bahai.org/library/authoritative-texts/abdul-baha/selections-writings-abdul-baha/
— *Some Answered Questions*. Haifa: Bahá'í World Centre, 2014. https://www.bahai.org/library/authoritative-texts/abdul-baha/some-answered-questions/
— *Tablets of Abdul-Baha*, vol. 3. Chicago: Bahai Publishing Society, 1916.
— *Tablets of the Divine Plan*. Wilmette, IL: Bahá'í Publishing Trust, 1993. https://www.bahai.org/library/authoritative-texts/abdul-baha/tablets-hague-abdul-baha/
— *The Will and Testament of 'Abdu'l-Bahá*. Wilmette, IL: Bahá'í Publishing Trust, 1991. https://www.bahai.org/library/authoritative-texts/abdul-baha/will-testament-abdul-baha/

Abdul Baha on Divine Philosophy. Boston: The Tudor Press, 1918.

'Abdu'l-Bahá in London. London: Bahá'í Publishing Trust, 1987.

The Bahá'í Faith 1844–1963: Information Statistical & Comparative. Compiled by the Hands of the Cause Residing in the Holy Land. Israel: Peli-P.E.C. Printing Works, no date.

Bahá'í Prayers: A Selection of Prayers Revealed by Bahá'u'lláh, the Báb and 'Abdu'l-Bahá. Wilmette, IL: Bahá'í Publishing Trust, 2002.

The Bahá'í World. vol. 13. Haifa: The Universal House of Justice, 1970.

Bahá'u'lláh. *Gems of Divine Mysteries: Javáhiru'l-Asrár*. Haifa: Bahá'í

World Centre, 2002. https://www.bahai.org/library/authoritative-texts/bahaullah/gems-divine-mysteries/
— *Gleanings from the Writings of Bahá'u'lláh*. Wilmette, IL: Bahá'í Publishing Trust, 1983. https://www.bahai.org/library/authoritative-texts/bahaullah/gleanings-writings-bahaullah/
— *The Hidden Words*. Wilmette, IL: Bahá'í Publishing Trust, 1990. https://www.bahai.org/library/authoritative-texts/bahaullah/hidden-words/
— *The Kitáb-i-Aqdas*. Haifa: Bahá'í World Centre, 1992. https://www.bahai.org/library/authoritative-texts/bahaullah/kitab-i-aqdas/
— *The Kitáb-i-Íqán*. Wilmette, IL: Bahá'í Publishing Trust, 1989. https://www.bahai.org/library/authoritative-texts/bahaullah/kitab-i-iqan/
— *The Proclamation of Bahá'u'lláh*. Haifa: Bahá'í World Centre, 1967.
— *Tablets of Bahá'u'lláh revealed after the Kitáb-i-Aqdas*. Haifa: Bahá'í World Centre, 1978. https://www.bahai.org/library/authoritative-texts/bahaullah/tablets-bahaullah/

Bediako, Kwame. *Theology and Identity: The Impact of Culture upon Christian Thought in the Second Century and in Modern Africa*. Oxford: Regnum Books, 1992.

'The Berlin Crisis, 1958–1961'. Office of the Historian. Foreign Service Institute United States Department of State. https://history.state.gov/milestones/1953-1960/berlin-crises

Bible, Holy. Various editions.

Century of Light. Commissioned by and prepared under the supervision of the Universal House of Justice. Haifa: Bahá'í World Centre, 2001. https://www.bahai.org/library/other-literature/official-statements-commentaries/century-light/

Clarke, Thurston. *Ask Not: The Inauguration of John F. Kennedy and the Speech That Changed America*. New York: Penguin, 2010.

The Compilation of Compilations. Prepared by the Universal House of Justice 1963–1990. vol. 1. [Mona Vale NSW]: Bahá'í Publications Australia, 1991.

'The Cuban Missile Crisis'. Office of the Historian. Foreign Service Institute United States Department of State. https://history.state.gov/milestones/1961-1968/cuban-missile-crisis

Dunbar, Hooper C. *Forces of Our Time: The Dynamics of Light and Darkness*. Oxford: George Ronald, 2009.

Ehrman, Bart. *The Orthodox Corruption of Scripture: The Effect of Early Christological Controversies on the Text of the New Testament.* Oxford: Oxford University Press, 2011.

Esslemont, John E. *Bahá'u'lláh and the New Era.* Wilmette, IL: Bahá'í Publishing Trust, 1980.

Fergusson, E. *Early Christians Speak: Faith and Life in the First Three Centuries.* Abilene, TX: Christian University Press, 1987.

Ferraby, John. *All Things Made New.* London: George Allen and Unwin, 1957.

Goodwin, Doris. 'The Way We Won: America's Economic Breakthrough During World War II'. *The American Prospect*, 19 Dec 2001. https://prospect.org/health/way-won-america-s-economic-breakthrough-world-war-ii/

Green, Victor H. *The Negro Motorist Green Book.* Self-published yearly in New York starting in 1940.

Hamilton, John Maxwell. *Manipulating the Masses: Woodrow Wilson and the Birth of American Propaganda.* Baton Rouge, LA: LSU Press, 2021.

Hogenson, Kathryn Jewett. *Lighting the Western Sky: The Hearst Pilgrimage and the Establishment of the Bahá'í Faith in the West.* Oxford: George Ronald, 2010.

Hollinger, Richard. *Community Histories: Studies in the Bábí and Bahá'í Religions*, vol. 6. Los Angeles, CA: Kalimát Press, 1992.

Hunt, Emily. *Christianity in the Second Century: The Case of Tatian.* New York: Routledge, 2003.

The Inter Ocean, 24 Sep 1893, pp. 650–1. https://www.newspapers.com/article/the-inter-ocean-1st-newspaper-mention-ba/309755/

Jenkins, Philip. '1968: 50 Years On'. Anxious Bench. Patheos. 27 July 2018 (updated 8 August 2018). https://www.patheos.com/blogs/anxiousbench/2018/07/fifty-years-on/

Jessup, Dr Henry H., quoting Bahá'u'lláh as recorded by E.G. Brown, in *World's Parliament of Religions*, vol. 2. Chicago: The Parliament Publishing Company, 1893.

Jones, Tony. *The Teaching of the Twelve: Believing and Practicing the Primitive Christianity of the Ancient Didache Community.* Brewster, MA: Paraclete Press, 2009.

Kelly, Joseph F. *The World of the Early Christians*. Collegeville, MN: Liturgical Press, 1997.

Kent, Stephen A. *From Slogans to Mantras: Social Protest and Religious Conversion in the Late Vietnam War Era*. Syracuse, NY: Syracuse University Press, 2001.

King, Karen L. *What is Gnosticism?* Cambridge, MA: Bellknap Press of Harvard University Press, 2003.

King, Martin Luther. *I Have a Dream: Writings and Speeches that Changed the World*. New York: Harper Collins, 1992.

Koehn, Jodi. 'East Germans Pressured Soviets to Build Berlin Wall'. Kennan Institute, Wilson Center, n.d. https://www.wilsoncenter.org/publication/east-germans-pressured-soviets-to-build-berlin-wall

Lang, Michael. *The Road to Woodstock*. New York: Harper Collins, 2009.

Makhani-Belkin, Tova. '"This Is a Progression, Not Conversion": Narratives of First-Generation Bahá'ís', in Momen and Heern, 'The Bahá'í Faith: Doctrinal and Historical Explorations', *Religions*, 2023, 14(3), 300. https://doi.org/10.3390/rel14030300; https://www.mdpi.com/2077-1444/14/3/300

Mariottini, Claude. 'Anasthatius and the Canon'. Blog posted 5 June 2007. https://claudemariottini.com/2007/06/05/athanasius-and-the-canon/

McLeod, Hugh. *Religious Crisis of the 1960s*. https://www.firstlutheransandpoint.org/1960–1970s.html; https://academic.oup.com/book/5409

— 'Why were the 1960s so Religiously Explosive?' *NTT Journal for Theology and the Study of Religion*, vol. 60, issue 2, May 2006, pp. 109–30. https://doi.org/10.5117/NTT2006.60.109.MCLE

'Military Spending in the United States', National Priorities Project, Institute for Policy Studies. https://www.nationalpriorities.org/campaigns/military-spending-united-states/

The Ministry of the Custodians, 1957–1963: An Account of the Stewardship of the Hands of the Cause. Haifa: Bahá'í World Centre, 1992.

Nakhjavani, Ali. 'The Ten Year Crusade'. *The Journal of Bahá'í Studies*. 14: 3/4. Ottawa: Association for Bahá'í Studies North America, 2004. https://bahai-library.com/nakhjavani_ten_year_crusade

One Common Faith. Commissioned by and prepared under the supervision of the Universal House of Justice. Wilmette, IL: Bahá'í Publishing Trust, 2005.

Park, Bum Jin, Yuko Tsunetsugu, Tamami Kasetani, Takahide Kagawa, Yoshifumi Miyasaki and Yoshifumi Myazaki. 'The physiological effects of shinrin-yoku (taking in the forest atmosphere or forest bathing): Evidence from field experiments in 24 forests across Japan.' *Environmental Health and Preventive Medicine 15*. Jed 5:18026; Environ Health Prev Med. 2010 Jan;15(1):18-26. doi: 10.1007/s12199-009-0086-9.

Pauwels, Jacques R. *Big Business and Hitler*. Toronto: James Lorimer and Co., 2017.

Petrus, Stephen. 'Rumblings of Discontent: American Popular Culture and its Response to the Beat Generation, 1957–1960'. *Studies in Popular Culture*, vol. 20, no. 1, Oct 1997, pp. 1–17. https://www.jstor.org/stable/23414596?mag=how-the-beat-generation-became-beatniks&seq=2#metadata_info_tab_contents

Principles of Bahá'í Administration. London: Bahá'í Publishing Trust, 1976.

Prudente, Tim. 'They went to prison for burning draft records'. *Los Angeles Times*. 5 May 2018. https://www.latimes.com/nation/la-na-catonsville-nine-20180505-story.html

Rabbání, Rúḥíyyih. *The Priceless Pearl*. London: Bahá'í Publishing Trust, 1969.

Richardson, Heather Cox. *How the South Won the Civil War*. Oxford: Oxford University Press, 2020.

Rohr, Richard. Center for Action and Contemplation. https://cac.org/about/our-teachers/richard-rohr

Rúḥíyyih Khánum. 'Message to Persian Baha'is abroad for "The Holy Year", 1992', given at the Bahá'í World Congress, New York. *Alaskan Bahá'í News*, 1993 and *Canadian Baha'i News*, vol. 5, no. 5. p. 6. https://bahaitalks.blogspot.com/2017/07/message-to-persian-bahais-abroad-for.html?fbclid

Shaw, Robert Gregory. 'Uncle Bill: A Personal Memoir'. https://bahai-library.com/shaw_uncle_bill_memoir

Shoghi Effendi. *The Advent of Divine Justice*. Wilmette, IL: Bahá'í Publishing Trust, 1990. https://www.bahai.org/library/authoritative-texts/shoghi-effendi/advent-divine-justice/

— *Bahá'í Administration*. Wilmette, IL: Bahá'í Publishing Trust, 1995. https://www.bahai.org/library/authoritative-texts/shoghi-effendi/bahai-administration/
— *God Passes By*. Wilmette, IL: Bahá'í Publishing Trust, rev. ed. 1995. https://www.bahai.org/library/authoritative-texts/shoghi-effendi/god-passes-by/
— *Letters of the Guardian to Australia and New Zealand*. Australia: Australian Bahá'í Publishing, 1971.
— *Messages to the Antipodes. Communications from Shoghi Effendi to the Bahá'í Communities of Australasia*. (ed. Graham Hassall). Mona Vale NSW: Bahá'í Publications Australia, 1997.
— *Messages to the Bahá'í World: 1950–1957*. Wilmette, IL: Bahá'í Publishing Trust, 1971.
— *Messages to Canada*. Thornhill, ON: Bahá'í Canada Publications, 2nd ed. 1999.
— *The Promised Day is Come*. Wilmette, IL: Bahá'í Publishing Trust, rev. ed. 1980. https://www.bahai.org/library/authoritative-texts/shoghi-effendi/promised-day-come/
— *The Unfolding Destiny of the British Bahá'í Community: The Messages of the Guardian of the Bahá'í Faith to the Bahá'ís of the British Isles*. London: Bahá'í Publishing Trust, 1981.
— *The World Order of Bahá'u'lláh*. Wilmette, IL: Bahá'í Publishing Trust, 1991. https://www.bahai.org/library/authoritative-texts/shoghi-effendi/world-order-bahaullah/

Stockman, Robert H. *The Bahá'í Faith in America: Origins, 1892–1900*, vol. 1. Wilmette, IL: Bahá'í Publishing Trust, 1985.

— *The Bahá'í Faith in America, Early Expansion, 1900–1912*, vol. 2. Oxford: George Ronald, 1995.

Taylor, Steve and Krisztina Egeto-Szabo. 'Exploring Awakening Experiences. A Study of Awakening Experiences in Terms of Their Triggers, Characteristics, Duration and After-Effects'. *Journal of Transpersonal Psychology*, vol. 49, no. 1, 2017.

'Tribute to Shoghi Effendi by Ruhiyyih Khanum', *Bahá'í News*, May 1958, no. 327, p. 6.

Universal House of Justice. To the Bahá'ís of the World, April 1964. https://www.bahai.org/library/authoritative-texts/search?q=1964#s=messages-universal-house-justice
— To the Followers of Bahá'u'lláh, 27 August 1989. https://www.bahai.org/library/authoritative-texts/the-universal-house-of-justice/messages/19890827_001/1#752147580

— To the Conference of the Continental Boards of Counsellors, 27 December 2005. https://www.bahai.org/library/authoritative-texts/the-universal-house-of-justice/messages/ 0051227_001/1# 527522699

— To the Baháʼís of the World, 28 November 2023. https://www.bahai.org/library/authoritative-texts/the-universal-house-of-justice/messages/20231128_001/1#973422615

'Vietnam'. John F. Kennedy Presidential Library and Museum. https://www.jfklibrary.org/learn/about-jfk/jfk-in-history/vietnam

Wagner, Walter H. *Christianity in the Second Century: After the Apostles.* Minneapolis, MN: Fortress Press, 1994.

Westman, Paul. *Walter Cronkite: The Most Trusted Man in America.* Minneapolis, MN: Dillon Press, 1980.

World's Parliament of Religions, vol. 2. Chicago: The Parliament Publishing Company, 1893.

References

Introduction
1. *Century of Light*, p. 52.
2. Universal House of Justice, in ibid.

1 Early Christians
1. King, *What is Gnosticism?*
2. Richard Rohr, Center for Action and Contemplation.
3. Shoghi Effendi, *God Passes By*, p. 331.
4. Shoghi Effendi, *Bahá'í Administration*, pp. 53–4.
5. Shoghi Effendi, *World Order*, pp. 168–9: 'To us, the "generation of the half-light", living at a time which may be designated as the period of the incubation of the World Commonwealth envisaged by Bahá'u'lláh, has been assigned a task whose high privilege we can never sufficiently appreciate, and the arduousness of which we can as yet but dimly recognize.'
6. Shoghi Effendi, *God Passes By*, p. 93. The biblical references are John 1.31, Luke 3:21–2, Mark 1:10–11, and Matthew 3: 16–17.
7. Acts 22:3.
8. Acts 5:38–9.
9. 'Abdu'l-Bahá, *Selections*, p. 163.
10. 'Abdu'l-Bahá, *Promulgation*, p. 134.
11. Bahá'u'lláh, *Gleanings*, p. 83.
12. Isaiah 63:10.
13. John 15.26 and Bahá'u'lláh, *Gems of Divine Mysteries*, para. 11.
14. Matthew 7:16.
15. Mariottini, 'Anasthatius and the Canon'.
16. ibid.
17. ibid.
18. See 'Abdu'l-Bahá, *Some Answered Questions*, no. 84, paras. 9 and 10.
19. Wagner, *Christianity in the Second Century*, p. 132.
20. ibid. p. 122.
21. Fergusson, *Early Christians Speak*, p. 34.
22. ibid. p. 14.
23. Wagner, *Christianity in the Second Century*, p. 121.
24. ibid. p. 122

25 Matthew 16:18
26 Bahá'u'lláh, *Kitáb-i-Aqdas*, para. 42.
27 Wagner, *Christianity in the Second Century*, p. 121.
28 Shoghi Effendi, *Promised Day is Come*, p. 110.
29 'Abdu'l-Bahá, *Selections*, pp. 223–4.
30 Shoghi Effendi, *World Order*, p. 20.
31 Kelly, *World of the Early Christians*, p. 181.
32 ibid.
33 Jones, *Teaching of the Twelve*, p. 136.
34 Kelly, *World of the Early Christians*, p. 182.
35 Bediako, *Theology and Identity*, p. 34.
36 ibid. p. 122 ff.
37 ibid. p. 17.
38 Hunt, *Christianity in the Second Century*, p. 16.
39 ibid. p. 13.
40 Wagner, *Christianity in the Second Century*, p. 157.
41 Hunt, *Christianity in the Second Century*, p. 59.
42 John 1:1.
43 'Abdu'l-Bahá, *Some Answered Questions*, no. 54, paras. 5 and 6.
44 Hunt, *Christianity in the Second Century* p. 129.
45 Tatian, *Oration*, ch. 13.
46 Hunt, *Christianity in the Second Century*, 139.
47 ibid. p. 156.
48 Ehrman, Bart. *Orthodox Corruption of Scripture*, p. 335.
49 See Bahá'u'lláh, *Kitáb-i-Aqdas*, para. 174 and note 184.
50 'Abdu'l-Bahá, *Will and Testament*, para. 16.
51 See, for example, letter of Shoghi Effendi to the National Spiritual Assembly of the British Isles, 14 November 1926, in Shoghi Effendi, *Unfolding Destiny*, p. 61.
52 Letter of Shoghi Effendi to Bahá'ís of the West, 12 February 1927, in Shoghi Effendi, *Bahá'í Administration*, pp. 120–3.
53 Richard Niebuhr, in Bediako, *Theology and Identity*, p. 33.

2 First Century American Bahá'ís

1 Shoghi Effendi, *Promised Day is Come*, p. 3.
2 Jessup, quoting Bahá'u'lláh as recorded by E.G. Browne, in *World's Parliament of Religions*, vol. 2, p. 1122.
3 See Stockman, *Bahá'í Faith in America*, vol. 1, pp. 13–31.
4 ibid. p. 16.
5 ibid. pp. 22–3.
6 ibid. p. 24.
7 ibid. p. 17.
8 ibid. pp. 17, 19.
9 ibid. p. 17.
10 ibid. p. 26.

11 ibid. pp. 30–1.
12 ibid. p. 66.
13 ibid. pp. 75–84.
14 ibid. pp. 81–2.
15 Stockman, *Bahá'í Faith in America*, vol. 2, p. 3.
16 See Hogenson, *Lighting the Western Sky*.
17 Stockman, *Bahá'í Faith in America*, vol. 1, p. 163.
18 ibid. p. 173.
19 ibid. p. 163.
20 *Century of Light*, p. 11.
21 Stockman, *Bahá'í Faith in America*, vol. 2, p. 392.
22 Hamilton, *Manipulating the Masses*.
23 Bahá'u'lláh, *Tablets*, p. 237.
24 Rabbání, *Priceless Pearl*, pp. 39–42.
25 ibid. p. 42.
26 ibid. p. 326.
27 ibid. p. 163.
28 'Tribute to Shoghi Effendi by Ruhiyyih Khanum', *Bahá'í News*, May 1958, no. 327, p. 6.
29 Shoghi Effendi, *Advent of Divine Justice*, p. 6.
30 ibid. p. 16.
31 *Century of Light*, p. 46.
32 ibid. pp. 46–7.
33 ibid. p. 46.
34 Pauwels, *Big Business and Hitler*.
35 Goodwin, 'The Way We Won'.
36 *Century of Light*, p. 46.
37 Kent, *From Slogans to Mantras*, p. 6.
38 Petrus, 'Rumblings of Discontent', pp. 1–17.
39 Shoghi Effendi, *Messages to the Bahá'í World*, p. 127.
40 ibid. p. 43.
41 Shoghi Effendi, *Advent of Divine Justice*, p. 16.
42 Bahá'u'lláh, *Gleanings*, p. 215.
43 Shoghi Effendi, *Messages to the Bahá'í World*, p. 7.
44 Nakhjavani, 'Ten Year Crusade', p. 11.
45 ibid. p. 12.
46 ibid. pp. 27–8.
47 *Ministry of the Custodians*, p. 8.
48 ibid. p.10.
49 ibid. p. 29.
50 ibid. p. 32.
51 ibid. p. 39.
52 Shoghi Effendi, *Messages to the Bahá'í World*, p. 127.
53 ibid. p. 169.
54 *The Bahá'í Faith 1844–1963*.

55 *Ministry of the Custodians*, pp. 231–6.
56 ibid. p. 321.
57 *Century of Light*, p. 43.
58 Shoghi Effendi, *World Order*, p. 170.
59 ibid.
60 Letter of the Universal House of Justice, April 1964.
61 'Abdu'l-Bahá, *Will and Testament*, p. 10.
62 Letter of the Universal House of Justice, April 1964.
63 ibid.
64 ibid.

3 The Sixties

1 McLeod, Hugh. 'Why were the 1960s so Religiously Explosive?'
2 Shoghi Effendi, letter of 11 March 1936, in Shoghi Effendi, *World Order*, p. 170.
3 King, *I Have a Dream*, p. 101.
4 Clarke, *Ask Not*, p. xvi.
5 Koehn, 'East Germans Pressured Soviets to Build Berlin Wall'.
6 'The Berlin Crisis, 1958–1961'.
7 The Cuban Missile Crisis.
8 *Century of Light*, para. 8.5.
9 'Vietnam'.
10 'Military Spending in the United States', National Priorities Project.
11 'Abdu'l-Bahá, *Selections*, pp. 103–4.
12 Shoghi Effendi, *Advent of Divine Justice*, pp. 19–20.
13 Jenkins, '1968: 50 Years On'.
14 Prudente, 'They went to prison for burning draft records', *Los Angeles Times*, 5 May 2018.
15 Jenkins, '1968: 50 Years On'.
16 Shoghi Effendi, letter of 11 Mar 1936, in Shoghi Effendi, *World Order*, p. 191.
17 Bahá'u'lláh, *Gleanings*, p. 213.
18 Bahá'u'lláh, *Epistle to the Son of the Wolf*, p. 31.
19 Bahá'u'lláh, *Hidden Words*, Arabic no. 2.
20 Westman, *Walter Cronkite*.
21 Bahá'u'lláh, *Epistle to the Son of the Wolf*, p. 31.
22 See Bahá'u'lláh, *Proclamation of Bahá'u'lláh*.
23 Bahá'u'lláh, *Gleanings*, pp. 250–1.
24 'Abdu'l-Bahá, *Promulgation of Universal Peace*, p. 232.
25 Westman, *Walter Cronkite*.
26 'Abdu'l-Bahá, *Promulgation of Universal Peace*, pp. 468–9.
27 'Abdu'l-Bahá, *Selections*, p. 247.
28 'Abdu'l-Bahá, *Promulgation of Universal Peace*, p. 316.
29 *Century of Light*, para. 8.7.
30 Bahá'u'lláh, *Hidden Words*, Arabic no. 16.

REFERENCES

31 Bahá'u'lláh, *Kitáb-i-Íqán*, p. 15.
32 From the description of Hooper Dunbar's book *Forces of Our Time*.
33 'Abdu'l-Bahá, *Tablets of Abdul-Baha*, vol. 3, p. 611.
34 Lang, *Road to Woodstock*, p. 246.
35 'Christian response to the revolutionary changes of the sixties is still evident. Some researchers say that contemporary music and a more relaxed, casual approach toward church are its major contributions. It was a turbulent and troubling time.' McLeod, *Religious Crisis of the 1960s*.
36 Shaw, 'Uncle Bill: A Personal Memoir', https://bahai-library.com/shaw_uncle_bill_memoir
37 'Abdu'l-Bahá, *Promulgation of Universal Peace*, pp. 253–5; *Some Answered Questions*, no. 83.
38 Bahá'u'lláh, *Hidden Words*, Persian no. 12.
39 Bahá'u'lláh, *Gems of the Divine Mysteries*, para. 17.
40 'Abdu'l-Bahá, *Paris Talks*, p. 17.
41 *Abdul Baha on Divine Philosophy*, pp. 160–1.
42 ibid. p. 122.
43 'Abdu'l-Bahá, *Paris Talks*, p. 163.
44 ibid. p. 85.
45 ibid. pp. 57–9.
46 'Abdu'l-Bahá, *Promulgation of Universal Peace*, p. 291.
47 'Abdu'l-Bahá, *Paris Talks*, p. 20.
48 'Abdu'l-Bahá, *Selections*, p. 302.
49 'Abdu'l-Bahá, in *Tablets of Abdul-Baha*, vol. 3, p. 562.
50 'Abdu'l-Bahá, *Promulgation of Universal Peace*, p. 107.
51 *One Common Faith*. Commissioned by the Universal House of Justice.
52 Universal House of Justice, Letter to the Conference of the Continental Boards of Counsellors, 27 Dec 2005.
53 'Abdu'l-Bahá, *Paris Talks*, p. 174.
54 'Abdu'l-Bahá, *Promulgation of Universal Peace*, p. 14.
55 'Abdu'l-Bahá, *Selections*, p. 63.
56 'Abdu'l-Bahá, *Promulgation of Universal Peace*, p. 22.
57 ibid.
58 Bahá'u'lláh, *Tablets*, p. 104.
59 'Abdu'l-Bahá, *Selections*, pp. 53–4.
60 'Abdu'l-Bahá, in *Abdu'l-Bahá in London*, pp. 104–5.
61 'Abdu'l-Bahá, *Paris Talks*, p. 17.
62 Richardson, *How the South Won the Civil War*.
63 'Abdu'l-Bahá, *Promulgation of Universal Peace*, p. 246.
64 'Abdu'l-Bahá, *Divine Philosophy*, p. 122.
65 *Abdu'l-Bahá in London*, p. 19.
66 ibid. pp. 54–5.
67 'All men have been created to carry forward an ever-advancing civilization.' Bahá'u'lláh, *Gleanings*, p. 215, no. 109.

68 'Signing a card' refers to an old system for keeping track of Baháʼí membership.
69 Taylor and Egeto-Szabo, p. 201.
70 Ferraby, *All Things Made New*.
71 Esslemont, *Baháʼu'lláh and the New Era*.
69 Makhani-Belkin, 'This Is a Progression, Not Conversion'.
72 '. . . seize, before the eyes of those who are in the heavens and those who are on the earth, the Chalice of Immortality, in the name of thy Lord, the Inaccessible, the Most High, and quaff thy fill, and be not of them that tarry.' Baháʼu'lláh, *Gleanings*, p. 148.
73 Baháʼu'lláh, *Gleanings*, p. 148.
74 Park, Bum Jin, et al. 'The physiological effect is shinrin-yoku'. *Environmental Health and Preventive Medicine*.

4 Second Century Believers

1 Shoghi Effendi, *Advent of Divine Justice*, p. 16.
2 From a letter written on behalf of Shoghi Effendi to an individual, 14 March 1932, in Shoghi Effendi, *Messages to the Antipodes*, p. 67.
3 *Century of Light*, pp. 47–8.
4 Green, *The Negro Motorist Green Book*.
5 Rúḥíyyih Khánum, 'Message to Persian Baha'is abroad for "The Holy Year", 1992', given at the Baháʼí World Congress, New York. *Alaskan Baháʼí News*, 1993 and *Canadian Baha'i News*, vol. 5, no. 5. p. 6. https://bahaitalks.blogspot.com/2017/07/message-to-persian-bahais-abroad-for.html?fbclid
6 *Century of Light*, p. 48.
7 From a letter written on behalf of Shoghi Effendi to the National Spiritual Assembly of the Baháʼís of Canada, 18 July 1957, in Shoghi Effendi, *Messages to Canada*, p. 264.
8 ʻAbduʼl-Bahá, *Paris Talks*, pp. 163–6.
9 Baháʼu'lláh, *Kitáb-i-Aqdas*, para. 149.

5 Truth, Community, Service, Spirit

1 ʻAbduʼl-Bahá, cited in a letter of Shoghi Effendi to the National Spiritual Assembly of Persia, 15 February 2022, in *Compilation of Compilations*, vol. 1, p. 97.
2 Baháʼu'lláh, *Tablets of Baháʼu'lláh*, p. 168.
3 From a letter of the Universal House of Justice, 27 August 1989.
4 'The Feast', https://www.youtube.com/watch?v=YSEOA2NuGfc
5 *Baháʼí World*, vol. 13, pp. 460–4.
6 Shoghi Effendi, in *Principles of Baháʼí Administration*, p. 1.
7 Baháʼu'lláh, *Tablets*, p. 141.
8 ʻAbduʼl-Bahá, *Promulgation of Universal Peace*, p. 94.
9 ʻAbduʼl-Bahá, *Selections*, p. 27.
10 Dunbar, *Forces of Our Time*, p. 6.

Afterword
1 'Abdu'l-Bahá, *Paris Talks*, pp. 57–9.

Glossary
1 Shoghi Effendi, *Letters from the Guardian to Australia and New Zealand*, p. 41.
2 Shoghi Effendi, *God Passes By*, pp. 210–14.
3 Universal House of Justice, letter to the Bahá'ís of the World, April 1964.
4 'Abdu'l-Bahá, *Promulgation of Universal Peace*, para. 130.8.
5 Bahá'u'lláh, *Gleanings*, p. 136.
6 'Abdu'l-Bahá, *Tablets*, vol. 3, p. 620.
7 'Abdu'l-Bahá, *Will and Testament*.
8 Shoghi Effendi, *World Order*, pp. 40, 203.

www.ingramcontent.com/pod-product-compliance
Lightning Source LLC
Chambersburg PA
CBHW022005160426
43197CB00007B/291